More Than a Game

The Best of Alf Van Hoose

EDITED BY CREG STEPHENSON AND ED MULLINS

A Publication of the College of Communication and Information Sciences and the Center for Community-Based Partnerships, The University of Alabama

THE UNIVERSITY OF ALABAMA PRESS
Tuscaloosa

The University of Alabama Press
Tuscaloosa, Alabama 35487-0380
uapress.ua.edu

Typeface: Perpetua

Cover design: Gary Gore

The editors acknowledge permission to reprint from the archives of the *Birmingham
News* and from materials, including photographs, made available to them by the family
of Alf and Carolyn Van Hoose.

Library of Congress Cataloging-in-Publication Data
Van Hoose, Alf, 1920–1997.
More than a game : the best of Alf Van Hoose / edited by Creg Stephenson and Ed
Mullins.
p.   cm.
"Fire Ant books."
Includes index.
"A Publication of the College of Communication and Information Sciences and the
Center for Community-Based Partnerships, the University of Alabama."
ISBN 978-0-8173-5511-1 (pbk.: alk. paper) — ISBN 978-0-8173-8109-7 (electronic)
1. Sports—Alabama. 2. Sports journalism—Alabama. 3. Van Hoose, Alf, 1920–1997.
I. Stephenson, Creg. II. Mullins, Edward, 1936–   III. University of Alabama. College of
Communication and Information Sciences. IV. University of Alabama. Center for
Community-Based Partnerships. V. Title.
GV584.A53V36   2009
796'.09761—dc22
                                        2009005078

This book is dedicated to everyone who read and enjoyed Alf Van Hoose's work through the years. Special thanks to Carolyn Van Hoose, Alf's wife, who helped us understand our topic and provided many of the photos and many leads to the ultimate content. Also to his daughter, Susanna Van Hoose Feld, who proofread the manuscript and wrote the foreword. Additional thanks go to Mark "Schuy" Van Hoose, who provided additional insight into his father's life and made several helpful suggestions regarding this book. Special thanks to Brad Guire for his assistance in the book's layout. Although we made no effort to duplicate the newspaper layout that professionally displayed Van Hoose's stories and columns, surrounded as they were with action photographs, bold headlines and—toward the end of his career—page after page of process color, we have followed most of the typographical conventions and AP style that characterize newspaper journalism. But it is the unique writing and powerful stories that are his legacy. And that is what we want to share in this book.

Contents

Foreword

Susanna Van Hoose Feld

My father was a very lucky man. He met, wrote about, befriended, and encouraged honest-to-goodness heroes. America's sporting life—the one place where you got paid for playing games—was also the one place where a fortunate few could get paid just for watching and writing about them. The richest man in the world could not buy what my dad enjoyed for more than half his life. But he never lost perspective on what the games should mean. They lighten hearts, lift spirits, and satisfy the gladiator urge in all of us. They give us spectacle, excitement, and drama; sports, above all, entertain.

To my dad, what sports were not about was war. He had seen both close up—too close up in war, which forged a more hardened man and dimmed, but never doused, his sunniness, his trust.

Once I asked him who was the greatest baseball player he ever saw. I anticipated Mickey Mantle, Sandy Koufax, Hank Aaron, Ted Williams. His answer: Josh Gibson. Who was he? What team did he play for? Was he still around? He was a catcher for the Homestead Greys, lifetime batting average .354, who died at age 36. I had forgotten about my dad's earlier assignment: scorekeeper for what was back then called the Negro Leagues. And so I realized that he had reached the zenith before I ever knew him, before our shared love of baseball bonded us in the sixties, when I was the only girl allowed to roam the roof of Rickwood during the long summer nights of that strange decade. I knew most of the fans, the regulars: the Bugler who played Taps for the visiting pitchers when they were pulled from the game; the greatest clown in baseball, Max Patkin, who mimicked the coaches and umpires like Groucho Marx; and the Landlady who let rooms in her boardinghouse to some of the A's and who always came on the bus and brought two tomato sandwiches to "watch my boys play." Daddy filled my life with characters. They all shared one bond: a love of the game.

One of the first sounds I recall is one I can only describe as a combination of crunching popcorn and a continual shredding and crinkling of aluminum foil, brief excited bits of voices, incoherent words, and then the crunching/crinkling would begin again until I fell asleep. I remember being in the car on trips to spring training and this sound lulling me to unconsciousness in the back seat. That this sound had a name—static—was a little disappointing because it had so much more in it. My dad searched through it like a prospector swirling for gold and finally finding a nugget—a game—on the radio where he easily interpreted the nonsense words and could instantly tell you, if you asked, "seventh inning, Cardinals just tied on a sacrifice."

I used to think that everybody's dad was like mine: that they all had a daily deadline, that every Sunday when the congregation prayed, they said, "forgive us our *off*enses" (opposite of *de*fenses), that every dad had (or would have if they could) a pocket-handkerchief garden. The one my father planted provided us with corn, tomatoes, beans, lettuce, radishes, turnips, carrots, and sometimes a watermelon. The neighbors benefited from Dad's largesse, plus they marveled at the sight of him leaning on his hoe—no royal gardener at Versailles ever gazed more thoroughly or more proudly at his creation than my dad looking over that small, vast corner of the yard.

Besides his travels to sporting events around the country, he made frequent trips to his hometown of Cuba, Alabama, a mile and a half from the Mississippi line. Cuba contained lifelong friends like Mayor Penny

Tate and Chief Upchurch, good fishing (usually with my brother Mark), and colorful stories. One of the funniest columns he ever wrote tells of a disastrous Cuba wedding beginning with the arrival of the brides-maids standing in the beds of pickup trucks so their dresses would not be wrinkled by sitting.

From Cuba in the fall of 1942 he boarded the train for War 2, as he called it, a trip that would take him, as an infantry captain in Patton's Third Army, to the easternmost limit of the Western Front. If Hitler had tried to flee to his southern redoubt at Berchtesgaden, my dad and his men were the ones positioned to take him. The Bastogne section of this book surprised our family when it was first published because he had never talked about the war itself. He didn't trust men who told of their heroic exploits. Didn't trust soldiers who wore their medals in peace-time. Never wore his Silver Star. Preferred to talk about his experiences with the army of occupation. Ran into Noel Coward in a London the-ater lobby between acts of someone else's play. Ingrid Bergman shook his hand on her goodwill tour.

He commanded the unit that guarded Neuschwanstein, the storied palace of mad King Ludwig of Bavaria, where the American soldiers in-spected the rooftop garden and explored the inevitable secret passage-ways. While he protected the castle, Dad did allow his soldiers access to the palace wine cellars where much conviviality reigned among those who sampled the 600-year-old bottles of wine. Before he came home, he visited Nuremberg and observed the trials. He was taken downstairs to see the German prisoners. Remembered Hermann Goering spitting at the officers who stared at him. It was only late in his life that I dared ask him if he had killed anyone in the war. Predictably, he answered me with silence. Whatever he did in combat, he left it there.

The legacies were wordless ones. All his life, my father paced. Only after reading the Bastogne stories did I realize that for a man who had been in too many foxholes under fire, the greatest freedom would be not to stay in one place too long. Extended patience also had been a war casualty as was a certain vulnerability. When President Kennedy was killed, my father cried—to me an event almost as terrible as the assassination.

But the most direct consequence, the most personal: my brothers and I became "the troops," his "gallant crew," and we performed many and various tasks and manual labors for Dad. To make it worse, our self-brevetted general vanished after giving orders and reappeared only after we finished the work. Desertion was not an option. Assembling a swing set, pouring a patio, finding anti-freeze for the car on Christmas Eve, the gallant crew could only hope for his highest praise: "You have done well." And then there were the war games. When it snowed, my brothers became the unlucky defenders of the snow fort, while I got to be on Dad's side. He drove the car slowly toward the target, both of us yelling, "Tank! Tank!"

The qualities he admired most were the ones he felt that General Patton, Shug Jordan, and Bear Bryant instilled in their men: respect, obedience, discipline, and victory. He kept the secrets. On the eve of the 1966 Orange Bowl, he got a dead-of-night call from Coach Bryant. "Can't sleep, Hoose. Can you come down and talk?" They talked about fishing and about squirrel hunting and about football. Toward dawn Coach Bryant told my dad that he had some surprises for the Nebraska Cornhuskers, and he proceeded to go over his game plan which included a more wide open offense. Later that day, quarterback Steve Sloan passed for an Orange Bowl record, and Alabama won Bryant's third national championship by a score of 39–28.

But all of the discipline and obedience were rarely enforced on Dad's grandson. Theirs was a mutual admiration society that brought to grandson Gil a rare high school graduation gift, a visit to the Birmingham Barons locker room where he sat in on a Yahtzee game with Michael Jordan. Gil also performed the primary duty of the first grandchild: christening the grandparents. My father became Burr, because of his pipe and the danger of ashes which might cause a "burn."

Daddy's pipe vexed the whole family, but me most of all. When I worked after college in the *Birmingham News* reference department, periodically a reporter would rush in and breathlessly inform me, "Your dad's on fire!" His thoughts somewhere out in a stadium, a battlefield, or a fish-laden lake, he had absently shoved his pipe into his back pants pocket and the effects had suddenly taken hold. I learned, after the first panic, that this was a customary occurrence—appearing as predictably as the All-Star game in July.

Well, I can hear his voice—ever the editor—over my shoulder, "Wrap it up, Sus, wrap it up." This is harder than he thinks. He never was a simple man though he loved simple things. Loved the game that different seasons brought, he loved the fans, he loved his readers, especially when they wrote to him—the pans as well as the praise. If you create a feeling strong enough for someone to write a letter, you've done your job, he said.

Satchel Paige, one of his favorite philosophers, advised that for a long and happy life, you should always "jangle softly as you walk." That was my Dad. In his pockets he kept pennies, keys, folded letters from friends, a worn black wallet containing often unidentifiable pictures of those he loved, tickets to somewhere, and the occasional smoldering pipe.

More Than a Game

Introduction

The Van Hoose style

Creg Stephenson

Although he spent more than 43 years at the same job, Alf Van Hoose was not a man limited by the boundaries of his profession.

The sports editor of the *Birmingham News* for 21 years and a columnist for a decade before that, Van Hoose helped define a city, a state, and a region largely known for sports. He was the writer of record covering some of the biggest sporting events and personalities in the state of Alabama in the last half of the 20th century.

Wayne Hester, Van Hoose's successor as sports editor of *The News* in 1990, said, "To many sports fans over the years, Alf Van Hoose has been the *Birmingham News*."

But he was also much more than that.

Born in 1920 and reared against the Alabama-Mississippi line in Cuba, Van Hoose grew up playing pasture baseball with dreams of becoming a major league player. After two years playing baseball and football and running track at Livingston State Teachers College (now the University of West Alabama), Van Hoose received his shot at a professional contract during a tryout with the St. Louis Browns. St. Louis scout Jacques Fournier, himself a former batting champion, told the shortstop Van Hoose that he had "big league hands" but lacked the bat speed for the majors.

Van Hoose turned down the contract at the behest of his father, Alf

Sr., who wanted his son to become a lawyer. The younger Van Hoose transferred to The University of Alabama in 1940 and became a journalism major because he wasn't interested in becoming an engineer, lawyer, or teacher, he later said.

While Van Hoose was in college, World War II broke out in Europe. He was drafted into the U.S. Army upon graduation in 1942 and wound up serving in the European theater, where he rose to rank of captain in famed Gen. George S. Patton's Third Army. Van Hoose saw action throughout France and Germany, most notably at the Battle of the Bulge, where he earned the Silver Star as head of a unit that rescued fellow soldiers from behind enemy lines (he had also won a Bronze Star for previous battle action).

After the war, Van Hoose served in the army of occupation in Austria until late 1946, when he returned home jobless and without an idea of what to do with his future. Through his younger brother, Jim (then himself a student at UA), Van Hoose met Charles Fell, Jr., the son of the managing editor of the *Birmingham News.*

That chance meeting led to an offer of $40 per week to become a writer under legendary *News* sports editor Zipp Newman, which Van Hoose accepted on March 24, 1947. By that time he had married longtime sweetheart Carolyn Eddins of Frisco City and would later become the father of two sons, Alfred III and Mark, and a daughter, Susanna.

Amazingly, a job at *The News* would be the only one Van Hoose ever had. He was a sports writer for 12 years, moving up to assistant sports editor and regular columnist under new sports editor Benny Marshall upon Newman's retirement in 1959. Van Hoose became sports editor when Marshall died 10 years later and held that position until his own retirement on April 1, 1990. (Newman, who among other things popularized the nickname "Alabama Crimson Tide," became sports editor of *The News* in 1919, meaning that in 61 years, the newspaper had only three sports editors.)

In all his time with *The News,* Van Hoose left the sports department on only three brief occasions. For a short time in 1958, he wrote a front-page news column titled "Vulcan" (after Birmingham's trademark statue overlooking the city). "'Vulcan' was a dream job, really," he told *The News* in 1990. "I could write about anything I wanted to. . . . But it was seven days a week, and that's a tough grind.

"I discovered people in sports were better people. Everybody who came to me while I was writing 'Vulcan' was hustling something. I think there are higher ethical standards in sports than any other part of society."

After eight months, Van Hoose was invited back into the sports department. He jumped at the chance, writing about his first love, baseball, as Birmingham Barons beat writer and assistant sports editor for 12 years until he became editor in late 1969.

Van Hoose stayed in sports for the rest of his career with two breaks. He left for three months in 1966 to cover the Vietnam War (he was chosen for the assignment by *The News* largely because of his combat experience). The second was for two weeks in 1989 to travel back to Europe and write a series of stories commemorating the 45th anniversary of World War II, particularly that part of the Battle of the Bulge that occurred around Bastogne, where Van Hoose had been stationed.

Unlike many of his contemporaries, forebears, and successors—many of whom might consider the *Sporting News* heavy reading—Van Hoose was a voracious reader. "He especially liked Thomas Wolfe," his wife, Carolyn, remembered.

In his University of Alabama days, Van Hoose studied under the famed creative writing professor Hudson Strode, who handpicked his students from among the brightest aspiring writers on campus. It was not unusual some years for Strode's entire class to eventually have a novel published, but it's hard to imagine that any of Van Hoose's fellow students would put as many words into print as he did.

Van Hoose wrote at least three columns a week in the *Birmingham News* for more than 30 years, and also wrote thousands of game stories and sports news pieces. Through the years, Van Hoose's columns were regularly peppered with literary references, from Shakespeare and Thornton Wilder to lesser known authors such as Antoine de Saint Exupéry. He made a habit of "limbering up" every two years by reading Tolstoy's epic *War and Peace*.

It is likely from this widely varied reading background that the Van Hoose style emerged, which is hard to describe. Well, let's leave that to famed author James Michener, who wrote in his 1976 tome *Sports in America*: "The smaller cities in the hinterland produce first-rate sports-writers, as I learned when I came to know Alf Van Hoose of the *Birmingham News*. In that sports-crazed town Van Hoose could get away with murder, writing as loosely as he cared; instead he produces some of the most compact and chiseled prose I have ever read on a sports page. His paragraphs are so tightly wound that they could have been written by a professor of English, one who was especially attentive to style."

Van Hoose often left out "unnecessary" words such as "a," "an," or "the" and was known to create his own words as well—casting into his paragraphs the likes of "jillion," as well as Southern colloquialisms such as "heckuva," "gonna," and shoulda." He loved the devices of parallelism and irony, often going several paragraphs into his columns before reaching the main idea (the "nut graph" in journalistic parlance).

In the 1983 story revealing the impending retirement of legendary Alabama football coach Paul "Bear" Bryant, Van Hoose went 126 words before mentioning the coach's name, instead describing different aspects of Bryant's career in a series of parallel sentences. His most famous lead turned on an ironic twist. Van Hoose's story from Game 1 of the 1954 World Series began by describing Birmingham native Willie Mays' famed catch as one "you had to see NOT to believe." (Although asked by his editors to do so many times, Van Hoose refused to enter any of his writing in state and national newspaper contests, because, as he told family members, he didn't want writing to be viewed as a competitive sport.)

Van Hoose's style was alternately loose and terse, both styles with an apparent design. Often his writing read like a telegram, in other cases like poetry. He was as comfortable writing in sentence fragments as he was in modifying a single noun or action verb with five or six adjectives or adverbs. That same story about Bryant's retirement included the following passage: "There were victories. Many, many. There were defeats. A few." On the other hand, he described Alabama's game-saving defensive stop in the 1979 Sugar Bowl against Penn State thus: "A barehanded, no-quarter-asked, primitive man-against-man goal line stand."

Like famed gossip columnist Walter Winchell before him, Van Hoose's writing trademark was the ellipsis. Many of his columns—and even some news articles—were stream-of-consciousness style strung together by ellipses. Witness the following passage from a 1976 column about the Alabama Sports Hall of Fame induction ceremony:

Small world department . . . Jackie Hayes was telling of the finest baseball game he ever saw, or participated in . . . It happened nearly 60 years ago, Eclectic beat Clanton, 1–0. Joe Sewell heard it.

"You may be right," Joe Sewell said, "Did you know I played in it, with Eclectic?"

Hayes didn't.

Van Hoose didn't consider his writing style flashy. He simply believed it was easier to read and understand, while still able to convey the mood of the events flashing before the writer's eyes. It certainly wasn't an ego thing.

"Most columnists write to impress other columnists," he told *Birmingham Magazine* in 1980, "but newspaper readers want to be informed and entertained in the simplest fashion."

In fact, Van Hoose went to great lengths to keep himself out of his own columns, referring more than once to "I" as "that most presump-

tuous of all letters." He also avoided using the stock phrase of the day—
"this reporter"—or its ilk.

When it was absolutely necessary to squeeze himself into the story,
he did so with great comic effect, as when he built an entire 1965
column (included in this collection) around a conversation with a spectator at a celebrity golf tournament. He reveals himself as a "pencil and
notebook man" and relays the words spoken in theatrical form, using
the pronouns "he" and "she" to identify the speakers.

Because he was a University of Alabama graduate and because of his
close friendship with Bryant over the years, Van Hoose was often ac-
cused of favoritism in the articles he wrote and in the amount of coverage his newspaper afforded the Crimson Tide. Michener noticed this,
writing, "When I pointed out to a friend in Alabama that Alf Van Hoose
seemed to be rather partisan where Bear Bryant and his Big Crimson
Machine were concerned, my friend replied, 'he damn well better be,
or we'd shoot him.'"

Largely because of Bryant, Alabama football dwarfed every other
sporting endeavor in the state during the time Van Hoose was sports
editor at *The News*. It only stands to reason that Crimson Tide football
would dominate the headlines.

For his part, "I am pro-Alabama," he told *Birmingham Magazine* in
1980. "But I'm also pro-Auburn, pro-Jacksonville State, pro-UAB and
pro-sports in this community. I want to see them all prosper.

"Of course, every decision on amount of coverage (column inches),
and position of a story is subjective and therefore subject to criticism.
A lot of fans from all schools try to remind me about ways I could have
been more objective and I accept their comments good-naturedly."

Though Van Hoose made light of accusations of partiality toward his
alma mater, he told those closest to him that it was important to him to
be neutral, to let events and actions, not personal bias, determine both
the amount of coverage and how it was played.

While his writing style may have been groundbreaking, Van Hoose
was most assuredly old school in his attitude toward the role of sports in

society. He stayed out of the "muckraking" that began to infiltrate newspaper sports sections in the 1960s and continues to this day.

"Sports are merely games played to entertain," he told *Birmingham Magazine*. "But they can't be taken lightly because they're important to a lot of people . . . I've always thought that our readers wanted to be informed and entertained when they read the sports section. That's why we look for positive stories to tell and leave the muckraking to others."

Sports figures noticed Van Hoose's gentleness of spirit, often giving him news tips they would not afford other writers. Most famously, Bryant allowed him to break the news of the legendary coach's retirement by telling him of his plans in a private conversation in Bryant's office late one night. While other writers were informed only of a press conference at the Alabama football complex the following afternoon, Van Hoose had a front-page article in that day's edition of *The News*.

It is for all these and many other reasons that the time has come to compile a collection of the "best of" Alf Van Hoose. Included here are a variety of his columns, sports stories, and other musings from his 43-year career at the *Birmingham News*.

This collection is divided into five sections, the first covering Van Hoose's early days on the job until he became a regular columnist in 1959. Following that is a sample of his Vietnam War coverage.

The largest section is that in the middle, which covers the bulk of Van Hoose's career—including his promotion to sports editor in 1969—up to the watershed event of Bryant's death in 1983. Following that is the final few years of Van Hoose's tenure, during which he did much reflection on his life and career.

The final section is Van Hoose's 45th anniversary coverage of World War II, for which he traveled back across the Atlantic and followed the path he and Patton's Third Army took through Europe for a week-long series that ran in December 1989. It was a fitting denouement to Van Hoose's career.

In the March 29, 1990, *Birmingham News* story announcing his retirement, Van Hoose told longtime colleague Jimmy Bryan he planned a busy retirement. "I'm going to write a book, I know," he said. "It'll have some of everything, sort of a reflective autobiography. Mostly I'll tell stories."

Unfortunately for us, Van Hoose never got around to finishing that book. A stroke suffered during the blizzard of 1993 left him bound to a wheelchair until he died following a heart attack on April 30, 1997, at the age of 76. He was inducted into the Alabama Sports Hall of Fame posthumously in 1999.

But he remained true to his promise to leave us with plenty of stories—47 years' worth. What follows is a handful of the best of those.

Some were chosen based on a list of most memorable stories Van Hoose revealed on the occasion of his retirement. Others were selected at the suggestion of his family or his legion of friends and admirers. Still some were chosen because of the importance of the events they described or simply because they were so magnificently written.

This is obviously not a comprehensive selection. It would take many books to hold every fine word Van Hoose crafted in his nearly half-century at the *Birmingham News*. The problem with compiling this book was not choosing what to put in but what to leave out.

In the last column he wrote before retirement, Van Hoose noted that he had written "an estimated 7,587" articles in his career. No one knows exactly how he came up with that number. His wry use of "an estimated" (as in "an estimated crowd of 78,000"), followed by a precise number, suggests that he was having some fun with a journalistic convention. But knowing his reluctance to embellish, we can be sure that this estimate, like everything else in his body of work, rested on solid reporting, with a little whimsey thrown in for good measure.

I
Early Days, 1947–1959

Van Hoose's first 12-plus years on the job saw him performing a variety of tasks in the sports department, as you would expect of a cub reporter.

In that time, Van Hoose covered many of the big football and baseball games around the state, as well as motor sports, outdoors, and golf. He also wrote a weekly golf notes column as well as a variety of feature stories (his light-hearted piece about Northport's baseball-playing Lary family is the first selection included here). In his spare time, he was official scorer for the Birmingham Black Barons of the Negro American League, where he cultivated a lifelong love of Rickwood Field, the home stadium of both the Black Barons and its white tenant, the Barons.

During his afternoons at Rickwood, Van Hoose helped "discover" a young Birmingham native named Willie Mays, who played as a high schooler with the Black Barons before being snapped up by the New York Giants. The second selection here is a column Van Hoose wrote in 1951 while subbing for the vacationing Zipp Newman (whose "Dusting 'em off" column ran five times a week), in which Van Hoose created a minor uproar by suggesting Mays was a better center fielder than Jimmy Piersall, then considered the finest player ever to play in Birmingham. (Piersall was in the midst of a Southern Association All-Star season that year and would soon embark on a flamboyant major league career, mostly with the Boston Red Sox.)

The column, which begins as a send-up of the ongoing dispute between Mobile manager Dixie Walker (a former major league star and longtime Birmingham resident) and Southern Association president Charlie Hurth before leading to the Mays vs. Piersall question, was the first opinion piece Van Hoose ever wrote for *The News*. Even though Mays was by then quickly establishing himself as a star with the New York Giants, imagine the fortitude it took in 1951 for a relatively young sports writer (Van Hoose was 31 at the time, but had been in the business only four years) going against his editor—who had been singing Piersall's praises all year—to suggest that a black man was a better player than the city's current white athletic hero.

Also included here is Van Hoose's coverage of the 1953 Master's, during which Ben Hogan set the event record for lowest aggregate score (since broken by Jack Nicklaus, Ray Floyd, and Tiger Woods twice). Van Hoose later called Hogan's weekend the greatest individual athletic performance he ever saw. Note in that piece his blend of reportage and interpretive journalism, a common practice of the day.

Notice also, as in the Auburn football game story from 1959 also printed here, that there is very little use of quotations by the participants in a given event. The sports writers of the time were expected to paint the picture of the events themselves.

However, there is a lengthy question-and-answer exchange in the story from the first game of the 1954 World Series—in which Van Hoose famously described Mays' catch as one that "had to be seen NOT to be believed."

This chapter also includes a few more of Van Hoose's early pieces, including a hilarious feature on journeyman pitcher Bobo Newsom, who, in addition to winning more than 200 games in the majors and nearly twice that in the minors, referred to both himself and everyone else as "Bobo." An otherwise routine report about a mediocre pitching performance becomes, in Van Hoose's hands, captivating reading when he allows Newsom's quasi-coherent ramblings to tell the story.

There is also the game story from one of the most famous events in Alabama basketball history—George Linn's near court-length shot against North Carolina in 1955. Note that Van Hoose measures the shot at 81 feet, not the 84 feet, 11 inches claimed by the Crimson Tide athletic department to this day and disputed by Van Hoose until he died. Consequently or not, he never covered much basketball once he became sports editor, often telling acquaintances that he felt the referees had too much control over the game for it to be enjoyable.

Van Hoose's first job after returning from his assignment writing "Vulcan" in 1958 was to cover the Birmingham Barons in their run to the first Southern Association championship in 20 years. His coverage of the championship game is included here as well.

—C.S.

Pitcher, Peach or Bass Horn Tooter?—Just Ask Mitt Lary, He's Got 'Em (1950)

Northport, Ala.—Looking for the best pitchers or peaches in Tuscaloosa County? Well, go six miles out from here on the Byler Road and start asking for Mitt Lary. Brother, he's got 'em.

The peaches he can deliver in a month. The pitchers today—by the half dozen.

There's Lefthander Joe. And Righthanders Raymond, Ed, Al, Frank and Gene.

Is Mitt (or formally, J. M.) proud of this crop of chunkers? To be sure, but he's not one to blow his own horn. He's got the only non-athlete in the family doing that—James, a former all-state bass horn man with Tuscaloosa County High.

Three of the Lary brothers are hurling with the University of Alabama. In the background of Alabama history are other famous baseball brothers, Dan and Ike Boone, Joe and Luke Sewell, but this is the first year the Tide has had three brothers on the same team.

But let's go back a bit to Mitt, father of seven, no girls. He's a native of Tuscaloosa County who went east early in life to seek his fortune. While working around New York and Boston, he had a tryout with the Red Sox in 1915. The Bosox passed him up and he was never to play pro baseball—just semi-pro.

In 1922 he came back to Tuscaloosa to start raising peaches and baseball players. Here's a summary on his boys:

Joe, 28, three-letter man at Tuscaloosa County High (all the boys went to the same prep school). Made varsity A's as pitcher at Alabama in 1945 and 1946. Pitches now with Central Foundry, Holt. Also working on his master's degree at the Capstone. Navy vet.

James, 26, non-athlete. Star bass horn man with County High. Army vet.

Raymond, 25, two-letter man in prep school. Army veteran of 10th Mountain Division. Played baseball in 1949 with Tuscaloosa Indians and Central Foundry. Now working with Goodrich Rubber Company, Tuscaloosa.

Ed, 23, three-letter prep man. Navy vet. Lettered on 1949 Alabama baseball and football teams. Should see action this week against Auburn or Ole Miss.

Al, 21, all-state football player with County High as fullback. Also played basketball and baseball. Two-year letterman as Tide end and accounted the best offensive end at Capstone since Don Hutson. Failed to letter as catcher on 1949 Tide diamond team but is attracting pro scouts as a fastball pitcher this year. Has won two and lost one, allowing only three runs in 27 innings.

Frank, 19, three-letter man as prepper but plays only baseball at Alabama. Labeled a sure-fire major league prospect, Frank is the ace of the Tide hurling staff although only a sophomore.

Gene, 16, captain-elect of County High's 1950 football team and ace pitcher for the school's present baseball team. There are those who think Gene will be the best athlete in the family.

Not only is Mitt concerned with his own boys, he works for other kids also. It was he who worked hardest in inaugurating the present Tuscaloosa County American Legion baseball program. That was in 1940.

Mitt won't say which is his favorite athlete among the family. That might cause too much argument around the Sunday dinner table when they all come back home.

Dusting 'Em Off (1951)

Made to order for the movies

Come in, Hollywood. It's your turn to take up the Dixie Walker case.

What a drama it was until George Trautman rang down the curtain yesterday to equal shouts of cheer and displeasure. The story's got everything. Listen, Hollywood:

Start your show with a heartless umpire dramatically waving righteous Dixie Walker and justice-seeking players off the field . . . Turn your cameras to the dressing room where amid tears, little Leroy Jarvis, the vicious plate-blocker, faints as full realization of the infamy of it all comes upon him.

The second act could take in President Charlie Hurth in air-conditioned comfort, smiling as he reads his ump's report. (Dixie Walker's letter could be shown on the richly-carpeted floor next to the wastebasket with a black footprint on it) . . . Show Dix getting word of his suspension in front of a mural depicting salt-mine life in Siberia in early January.

The third act would be terrific. After Dixie has worn gaping holes in his shoe leather, he takes his hat in hand and enters the final tribunal.

Trautman's simply furnished office . . . Speed up the cameras to show Trautman in action, calling a quick trial, ordering Hurth, Roy and Paul Chervinko to court.

The climax scene is a natural. Bring your "Gone With the Wind" sets up to date and have millions carrying Dixie down Peachtree Street, clutching a white parchment with the word PARDON written on it in bold, black letters.

Are you listening, DeMille?

Trautman Had Solid Precedent (1951)

Whatever the merits of the Dixie Walker case (which Southern League fans will argue for moons to come), George Trautman had solid precedent in his overrule of Charlie Hurth.

The highest baseball figure, Commissioner Kennesaw M. Landis no less, once reversed Southern League President John D. Martin's decision on a makeup game and it meant Chattanooga won its only pennant.

Remember the September case of 1932? Not many do. Therefore here's the Reach Baseball Guide's version of the affair:

As the schedule drew to a close, Chattanooga was left with two games to play and Memphis with three and if both won all games, Memphis would win by a point.

It happened, however, that Chattanooga had one game with Knoxville unplayed, left over from Labor Day when darkness halted a second game with the Smokies in the third inning. The series between the two teams, as far as Chattanooga was concerned, was closed and President Watkins of Memphis contended that the time for playing a postponed game had passed although President Martin of the Southern Association had ruled that the game might be played.

The board of directors of the league, however, overruled Martin's decision who thereupon reversed his former decision.

President Joe Engel of Chattanooga appealed the case to Commissioner Landis who decided that inasmuch as Little Rock and Knoxville had played off a game after their series had closed, a precedent had been established and ruled the game was legal.

The announcement necessitated action . . . and a hurried trip from Knoxville put the teams in Chattanooga later than the regular starting hour but with sufficient time to play six innings. Chattanooga won and also took the two remaining games in Knoxville.

In the meanwhile Memphis had New Orleans for its opponent and vanquished the latter in three games straight but percentage was inexorable. The two points that Chattanooga obtained loomed up as a monument to "what might have been."

Two other things might be interesting in the famed case. In the "games behind" column of the standings, Chattanooga finished half a game behind Memphis. The Chicks that year won 101, lost 53. Chattanooga won 98, lost 51.

Another thing was that Chattanooga, sparked by such fellows as Cecil Travis, Dutch McColl and Harley Boss, easily won the Dixie Series from Beaumont in five games. Playing first base for Beaumont was a gangling kid famed as a "good hit, no field."

The kid was Hank Greenberg. Remember?

Mays vs. Piersall—Mays (1951)

To those who contend Jim Piersall is the finest center fielder in Birmingham baseball history, a word of caution: Was he superior to the Willie Mays the New York Giants bought from the Birmingham Black Barons in May, 1950?

You can get a good argument from observers of the two.

Had this reporter to rate the two defensively, here's the chart:

Speed—Piersall (picture finish).
Range—Tie.
Break—Piersall (squeaky vote).

Hustle—Mays.
Alertness—Mays.
Throwing—Mays.

Mays outthrow Piersall, you ask? Did you ever see Mays take a wall ball in right center and aim at third? Or retreat in center field for a fly ball and dare a runner on third to become ambitious? If you haven't, reserve judgment.

Piersall should easily lead Southern center fielders in assists. Mays is not too bad a bet to do the same in the National League although he must guard the deep reaches of the Polo Grounds.

As regards Mays' throwing, it might be pointed out that before the Giants paid $15,000 for him (a record price for his league), scouts trailing him saw him clearest as a future pitcher. Bill Maughn, watching him in the interest of the Boston Braves, often said, "That guy is a pitcher. With his loose form, he could throw all day. And hard."

There has been very little written about Mays' defense work since he was recalled by the Giants. He's struck too many home runs after such a stumbling start (one hit in 26 times at bat).

Black Baron fans are amazed at his outburst of power. Although he batted fourth in the lineup here, he was not regarded as a distance man. They figure he could carry the glove of any center fielder in the majors but were doubtful of his bat.

Now that he's hitting regularly, it's hard to see Mays otherwise than a major league star for many years to come.

Bobo Talks it Over—"Didn't Have My Regular Stuff" . . . but He Had Enough (1951)

"I'll tell you, Bobo," said the tremendous fellow pulling off a sweatshirt he could have dried by pitching in a lake. "Ole Bo didn't have his regular stuff out there tonight . . . Four runs, I give up, Bobo. Why that's the most a team's got off Bo in two months."

The big fellow shucked his shirt and continued court:

"That was the ninth straight, wasn't it, Bobo?" The sentence was punctuated with a giant wink.

Bobo Newsom was right. His last loss came on a 2–0 setback, June 14, by the same Memphis crowd which staggered the big guy several times last night but wasn't able to get the count to 10. 5–4 win was his 13th of the season.

Newsom asked for a cold drink and a clubhouse boy ran to get it.

"Naw, Bobo, I didn't quite have my stuff tonight," he repeated, which reminded him to yell at a relaxing Red Marion.

"Say, Red, you're gonna leave me something in your will. Pitching an old guy like me with only two days rest."

The quick Marion smile preceded a reply. "Remember you in my will? I hope you leave me a piece of your will."

Newsom's jibe took Marion's mind briefly from worrying about his club and its chances in the Little Rock chase which ends in five weeks.

"If we can only go to hitting," muttered the redhead. "If we can just start hitting."

Did he think the club could overhaul the Travelers?

"If we can help our pitchers, we could," said the boss. "That was a good ball George hit, wasn't it?"

Marion was referring to Wilson's blow into the Negro bleachers. The Baron clotheshorse flogged a pitch 12 rows up, a liner which zoomed out of the park over the 350-foot mark. It broke a minor slump the Kid had fallen into in the Little Rock series.

Blows like Wilson's give hope to Marion that the club will keep the pressure on the Travelers. Jim Piersall has trailed slightly lately but the great centerfielder should bounce back.

As Marion and Bobo talked, the same Piersall was dressing silently across the bench. A bandage the size of second base covered a sliding abrasion on his hip, a little mark of the trade he picked up while breaking up a Trav double-play. And Piersall is down 15 pounds to 167. The heat is wearing on the Connecticut youngster.

But a fellow can't spend too much time worrying about weight reductions around Bobo.

You've got to worry with him about hitters. Take the case of Bill Higdon who sent a Newsom curve to the top of the bleachers.

"How'd he pull that ball?" asked Bobo. "It was a curve ball. I knew it was gone."

Newsom will have time to ponder his question before his next assignment. He will go again Tuesday night against New Orleans and then against Little Rock in the do-or-die series.

"You're gonna work me, my night, aren't you, Red?" he asked. "Let's see, Tuesday, Wednesday, Thursday—it ought to fall right."

Newsom was referring to Blooper Ball night scheduled for him Saturday, Aug. 31. You'd think a guy who's been around as much as he would take such things in stride. But evidently Ole Bo was proud that folks were remembering him.

He hopes to win his 11th straight that night.

Dusting 'Em Off (1952)

A fellow learns city ways.

I've learned a lot of things since I came to town.

Back in Cuba, Ala., we used to call it dinner when the peas, the butterbeans, okra, buttermilk, cornbread and 20-cents-a-pound round steak was spread out sometime around high noon. We were wrong.

What we were really eating was lunch and the leftover that followed that evening (as surely as sundown) was dinner.

I've learned something else. I've learned a game called golf . . . a thing that leads straight to the psychiatrist's couch if not checked.

Back in the country I was completely ignorant of the straight left arm, the wristy follow-through and other secrets of a cult of pros who in other (and maybe better) days would have probably sold medicine off the back of a wagon.

Another thing I've learned in town. The baseball we played back in

Cuba, York, Livingston, Emelle and Bellamy, was strictly rural stuff. A branch brand. Far inferior to the sophisticated style of more populated precincts.

All in all, I guess our baseball grade was inferior. But for the life of me, I can't adopt the brand I see today to my heart while divorcing the style of 15 years ago.

I can't understand why small town baseball is dying. It was a great sport, for both citizen and player.

The citizen got his exercise first. It was only the nimblest and slyest who could evade the big guy (sometime the manager) working his way through the crowd with an open John Ruskin cigar box. He expected a donation but if he averaged 15 cents a head, he counted it a brilliant day.

For the Big Games, Paid Players

Once the box office was shut, you could expect the game to get under way soon. Not always. Sometimes there were tardy players due to an uncooperative mule which didn't understand it was about to get a few hours off as soon as the north-cut cotton patch was plowed.

If a big game was on tap on this Thursday afternoon (Thursday because that was store-closing day) there might be a hired player among the starters.

These semi-pros were mostly employed because of prowess with the bat. They were not glove men, as most seemed to run to large size. Except for the big gap they filled at first, third or the outfield, they turned over the balls hit to their right or left to more active teammates.

These guys were bought (and sometimes paid as high as 10 bucks per game) simply because they had been known, on occasion, to flog one into the cornfield back of right field, or beyond Mr. Rye Shaw's pasture fence in left.

But, by and large, the hometown team were hometown boys, or boys on the local rural route.

The umpire's authority was more or less a fleeting thing. Umpires were usually townsmen, non-paid, who in the midst of battle, though not becoming partial, might be counted on to lean the right way. Sometimes the visiting teams brought their ump. In these cases the visitor was assigned the less-important base posts while the home-towner kept his spot behind the pitcher's mound.

Duty-Bound to Go the Route

There were no platooning players. A pitcher was expected to go nine, a lefthanded batter was expected to hit a lefty and a fielder was expected to handle everything he got his hands on. If he touched the ball and missed, error.

There was little strategy, all offense. If a fast man got to first, he was expected to steal second. And often third. If a man was on first, a teammate on third, the back runner was expected to go to second unmolested on the first pitch. The catcher seldom threw.

Once in a while someone would go outside the rules, the rules according to the home team.

I remember a dastardly trick once pulled by Vardaman Catlett, the Ward, Ala., leftfielder. Playing in Ward, Cuba slugger Robert Wilson hit one over the fence into the cotton patch. (Over the fence meant nothing except to run.)

Wilson thought he'd run it into a homer but how wrong he was. Catlett leaped the fence, knelt among the boll weevils and pulled another ball from his pocket. Wilson was out at the plate in a sliding cloud of dust. Cuba lost, 10–9.

Years later, Catlett confessed.

That was a sad night in Cuba when Wilson was thrown out. But there had been sad ones before.

One came after a crucial game with York. The tying run was on third, the winning one on second. The batter took two strikes. The next pitch was two feet outside.

There was no hesitation, the batter swung—and missed.

As the crowd trudged away to Fords, Chevrolets and horses, a big farmer walked over to the dejected, disgraced batter and offered immortal words: "You shoulda let that one went, son, you shoulda let that one went."

Ben Hogan Takes Charge in Masters with Sizzling 66, Four-Stroke Lead (1953)

Augusta, Ga.——Ben Hogan's brilliant 66 just about broke up the party of the world's greatest golfers here Saturday.

The show goes on Sunday with the first 18-hole act scheduled but there are few who believe the sturdy little ex-Texan can be caught.

He owns a four-stroke lead over the field and has the incentive to break the Masters Tournament record of 279.

Taking four strokes from Hogan can be compared to snatching a T-bone steak from a dieting tiger.

After three rounds Hogan had cards of 70-69-66——205. A 73 Sunday will give this tournament a new low mark and would in all probability assure (a) his second Masters championship, (b) big cup and handshake from Bobby Jones, and (c) the greatest cheer ever heard here for a job well done.

Hogan said after Saturday's six-under-par record that "I believe a new record will be set." He didn't say who would do it. Didn't have to. Everyone in the locker room knew the man of whom he spoke.

Ed Oliver Second

Second to Hogan after three rounds was Ed Oliver, co-pro with Hogan at Seanky Course in Palm Springs, Cal. Oliver has 209, 67 strokes of which came Saturday while playing with and almost matching his partner, birdie for birdie.

In third place at 210 is Bob Hamilton of Evansville, Ind. Hamilton had third straight sub-par round Saturday, 70, but continued to lose ground to a Hogan whose putter finally warmed up with the rest of his equipment.

The rest of the field is strung out to the 240 unfortunately owned by Olin Dutra of Mexico City.

Hope Is Faint

Lloyd Mangrum is alone at 213. Tommy Bolt, Al Besselink and Ted Kroll are bunched at 214. They could catch Hogan or Oliver or Hamilton but hope is faint.

Disappointedly behind the leaders at 217 is Hogan's old foe, Sam Snead. Snead made as if to look Mr. Hogan in the eye Saturday by cutting par a stroke on each of the two first holes but he couldn't keep the pace.

The Slammer kept trying, however, and his one-under-par 71 was good stuff—but not the kind of stuff needed to overhaul Hogan.

Hogan early gave indication that this beautiful Georgia Saturday needed something special for spice. Trapped on the 355-yard second hole, he exploded to within 12 feet of the flag; he then dropped the first of seven birdie putts.

His second bird was bagged at three feet—or point-blank range—it came after he slammed a three-iron shot close to the pin on 220-yard No. 5.

He undercut par again on the 520-yard hole with two smashed wood shots and a pair of putts.

On nine he rushed in one of the longest putts in the tournament—a 50 footer if it was an inch; it gave him a three and a front side of 32.

Another long putting tap, this one on the tough par-four 10th hole, meant he was five under. This nudge gently disappeared in the ground after a winding journey of about 35 feet.

4,000 Gallery

Hogan's gallery (which must have been 4,000) began to scent a new course record when the man it was tracking got on the treacherous par-five 13th hole in two. Hogan, himself, was taking a run at the 64 of Lloyd Mangrum. He normally plays this hole to get on in three and avoid possible encounter with the guarding ditch.

But the dull bald putter which had stood Hogan so nobly thus far, failed him here. Hogan three-putted from 36 feet. His first try was short by four feet and his next try neatly evaded the cup at the last second.

The crowd groaned. But birdies on the next two holes had it cheering again.

The first of this pair followed a five-foot putt on No. 14, the second came after Hogan gambled and won the green with his second shot across the lake protecting the par-five No. 15 flag.

The man was now seven under par—one more birdie and he was set up for a 64.

But the 64 he envisioned turned to a 66 when he three-putted the 16th green. Again his approach putt was four feet shy, again his second try ran outside the cup.

He couldn't better par the last two holes.

Three-putting notwithstanding, it was still Hogan's best round over this 6,900-yard layout. Maybe not as thrilling as the 68 he shot to win the 1951 tournament but still his low score.

As Hogan went to the locker room to relax he attributed the fine weather and helpful east breeze as major factors in his 66. The wind (though not at all heavy) was behind him on three of the par-five holes.

Oliver's card showed an eagle, six birdies, eight pars and three bogeys.

The eagle followed a 25-foot putt on No. 13. The birdies came on putts ranging from 25 to two feet.

The bogeys all resulted from three-putting slick greens.

Hogan and Oliver had a best ball card of 6, 12 under par—pretty good for guys from Wilmington, Del., and Fort Worth, Tex., who went West last year to mine golf gold in California.

'Bama Day in Old New York (September 30, 1954)

Polo Grounds, New York, Sept. 30—Yankee journalists might call it discrimination but what was Wednesday at this Mathewson-McGraw and Hubbell-memoried park if it wasn't Alabama Day?

Fabled Willie Mays saving the hour in the eighth with a catch you had to see NOT to believe . . . Pinch-hitting Dusty Rhodes winning it in the 10th with a homer.

· Sho, suh, it took some more Giants to whip those Cleveland Indians, 5–2, a heap more Giants, but the delegates from Alabama did the dirty stuff—our Willie Mays on option to the Giants from Fairfield; our old Dusty in the big town on leave from Montgomery.

You shoulda seen the way the picture-takers and news reporters ganged Mays and Rhodes in the green, upstairs, clubhouse after it was all over.

The clubhouse is pea-patch distance from home plate, but just back of the spot where Say-Hey Willie flew back in the eighth for one of the great catches of all time.

The Giants were celebrating like winning politicians. Everybody was trying to talk at once . . . everybody, that is, 'cept Mays. Mays had escaped temporarily to the showers. He had spotted newsmen and photographers coming . . . Rhodes was caught with his shirt on. He hadn't tried hard to get away; he was most proud of his day's work, naturally.

What was it you hit, Dusty?

"A curve," answered Rhodes, "a high curve . . . It came in fat . . . I had gone up with the idea of taking a pitch. I couldn't do it—the thing was too pretty."

You didn't hit it good, did you Dusty, someone else asked. (The homer was honestly as Chinese as a Shanghai laundry ticket; a tall pop fly which crawled into the stands just down the rightfield line about the 270-foot mark.)

"Didn't hit it good?" replied Dusty. "Man, I must have hit it 400 feet—400 feet straight up." And he laughed big.

Did it worry Dusty to go up "cold" as a pinch hitter?

"Worry me? No, sir. It ought to worry the pitcher to get me out. He's got the big job, not me."

By this time Mays was back in sight, wearing towel and best TV smile.

Some photographer ambushed him and escorted him over to Dusty for a Heroes, Inc., shot. The other picture boys seemed to like the idea. Willie had to do, then re-do the routine which was removing Dusty's cap.

Mays then headed to dress in the far corner of the room. He tracked water past Leo Durocher, who was telling a huddled ground of reporters that Willie's catch wasn't the best ever.

"He's made a lot like that," whispered Leo in a laryngitis tone. "How can you pick out the best? Nothing he does surprises me anymore . . . He's the greatest."

When the hubbub dies around Mays, some 10 minutes later, long after he frankly told everybody that he knew he could make the play "Because I thought it was gonna stay in the ball park," Willie admitted he had practiced such a catch, often.

"I spent a lot of time in spring training working on that going away, over-the-shoulder catch," he said. "It's the toughest an outfielder has to make.

"I looked back once after (Vic) Wertz hit the ball and I knew it was going far out. I just kept running and the next time I glanced around, there the ball was, I took it over my left shoulder.

"It wasn't nothing to be too proud of, not when you go 0 for 3 for the day."

Actually Mays had only a routine afternoon until the eighth-inning clutch defensive situation came.

In the first he had popped up, with men on first and third. In the third he had walked, pushing Don Mueller into scoring territory for Henry Thompson's game-tying single to right.

In the fifth and seventh he had grounded out, not too sharply.

Except for his catch in the eighth, Mays never would have had an overtime batting chance in the 10th—an opportunity he used to coax a walk on five pitches.

Bob Lemon couldn't gamble on throwing anything fat to Willie, Willie knew it. And Lemon knew a pitch later that he couldn't gamble on pitching to Thompson—after Mays had stolen second in a cloud of sliding dust and a lost cap.

So Lemon put Thompson on purposely.

Leo then sent Dusty to the plate.

It was all over in three seconds.

TV cameras probably weren't focused on Mays during the flight of Rhodes' hit. They usually try to follow the ball.

For those who'd like it straight on Willie, as the ball floated lazily downwind, he was leaping up and down a few feet past second.

He had to be bodily pushed back to the base-path by Mueller to lead the winning, three-run production home.

Go-Go Tidesmen Start Mission Anew as Linn Sinks 81-Foot Basket (January 6, 1955)

University, Ala., Jan. 5—Confidently maintaining "we're better," Johnny Dee's go-go, throw-throw Alabama basketball team started the second leg of the year's mission today.

Non-conference stuff is finished, 10 games of it. Conference work is ahead, 14 games, the time to go at Kentucky growing mightier by the hour.

The first act ended last night, successfully, sensationally.

Successful on an 8–2 victory note. Sensational because straight and faraway shooting whipped a good North Carolina team last night, 77–55, such distance firing including an 81-foot basket by George Linn which kept a capacity Foster Auditorium audience buzzing for five minutes of halftime.

You read it right: 81 feet, Ozark Ike style, an over-the-head fling by Linn which arched downcourt, banged against the glass backboard, and dropped through the hoop cleanly, but not silently. The crowd was on its feet by that time, cheering a feat comparable to Mickey Mantle's 563-foot home run or Willie Mays' catch of Vic Wertz's 465-foot drive.

It set off a scramble through record books and memory. Unofficially the SEC distance mark is 64 feet, 7-1/2 inches, by Kentucky's Cliff Barker against Vanderbilt in 1949. That would have been from just behind center circle, just a summertime throw compared to Linn's.

Linn took a rebound directly under the Tarheel board, dribbled quickly twice and let her fly. Alabama didn't need the goal but it serves as a hint of how last night's contest was won.

From the field Alabama was 49.3 percent accurate, 34 of 69 shots. North Carolina was bigger in the rebounding area but Linn, Leon Marlaire, Dennis O'Shea and Jimmy Harper sidetracked that advantage. They just threw the ball through the cords. There's no rebounding necessary after that.

Linn, working his one-handed shot from around the circle—and that high-hard one from far downcourt—dropped in 21 points. That led things for the winners. Marlaire and O'Shea followed with 14 apiece. Jim Bratton, flitting here and there, got home nine points, a career high.

Jerry Harper, usually the Tide bellcow, was held to six points. Let that fool no one, however. He had a good night, feeding to the outside, rebounding (18 of 'em) inside. He's in no slump.

Soph Leonard Rosenbluth, a 6-5 Greenville, Tenn., forward on a team heavily-loaded with New York and Jersey men, threw in 21 points for a Tarheel cause behind from the start. He couldn't be stopped by the Tide, but his mates could. They couldn't shake free enough from a shifting, dogging Bama defense.

Actually the Tide was never in trouble. Off to a 8–0 advantage, the home lads ran it to 15–6 in six minutes.

The Tarheels briefly made a fight of it there. Rosenbluth popped in two outsiders, and two foul throws. Jerome Vayda added a crip. Anthony Radovich pushed through a jump shot—and the spread was down to 17–16, Alabama.

Good time ended suddenly for the visitors. Marlaire hit two long ones, O'Shea another, and Alabama was en route to a 40–29 halftime advantage.

At the three-quarters pole, Bama was 58–34, rolling smoothly along, and three minutes later (when it was 64–36) Dee pulled his big team. The subs took over and brought the thing in without too much trouble.

Auburn Defenses Vols to Death (1958)

Lamar Rawson and Tommy Lorino blew in for touchdowns Saturday, but it was not slick-footed running which notified the nation Saturday that mighty Auburn was shooting straight again at No. 1 U.S.A.

As 37,000 watched from Legion Field perches, millions more on countrywide TV, Shug Jordan's superbly conditioned Tigers battered and bruised and brutally busted Tennessee, 13–0. The Vols didn't make a first down.

It took 45 minutes for Auburn's offense to break away, but Hal Herring's defense never rested. It kept working, working, working, and finally it was Tennessee's fourth-quarter reputation which exploded. But for that no one blamed a soul. Even Corregidors fail.

Giant Jerry Wilson, Zeke Smith, Cleve Wester and Mike Simmons laid waste to Vol single-wing attacking and the Vols ended the day 30 yards in the hole. Runningwise, it was 49 yards of deficit.

A la Larsen

Tennessee's no-first-down performance must surely rank in futility with Yankee Don Larsen's perfect no-hitting the Brooklyn Dodgers in 1956. Auburn was simply masterful rolling its unbeaten, untied string to 15 games, longest in the land.

Rawson scored his touchdown sweeping end for four yards, five seconds into the final quarter. Lorino followed him into the north end zone five minutes later, from the 24.

The slick and stylish halfbacks took pitchouts from steady, scholarly Lloyd Nix, director of Auburn's multiple offense.

Wind a Factor

Offensive strategy was dictated muchly by a 15-mile wind—maybe from Hurricane Helene—whipping in from the northwest. The Vols used it to bottle Auburn the first quarter, and then fought evenly against it until halftime.

Auburn rode the breeze in the third quarter, but it didn't turn the tide. Those big white-shirted linemen, attacking in the manner of hungry beasts, did.

Tennessee, its old and trusted attack plans in the hands of rookie tailback Billy Majors and veteran Danny Webb, was humiliated on offense.

The Vols did much better when Auburn had the ball, their slashing, knifing tackling might have discouraged a less-worthy foe.

Lorino, kept in check inside, finally was unhalted late by Nix and dispatched wide. Little Tommy then rushed his total of 59 yards for eight tries, high for the hot, humid afternoon.

Nix finished gaining runner-up to his flashy buddy, 35 yards in 10 attempts. Thirty-two yards of Nix's net came in Auburn's magnificent roll to a first touchdown.

Better Troops

Jordan out-platooned losing Bowden Wyatt but maybe because he appeared to have better young troops. Auburn unveiled some young lions in sophomores Ed Dyas, Ken Rice, Leon Myers, Jimmy Pettus and G. W. Clapp.

Dyas, a child star just 18, now must take over as top-team when full regular Ronnie Robbs went limping away with a bad leg.

He may be out six weeks.

The shattering Dyas did 31 yards in six surges. He's not as quick off the mark as Joe Childress—who is?—but when he hits, he hurts.

Auburn was favored by nine points but Tennessee came hoping to defrock the SEC and national king. Legion Field has long been happy Vol hunting ground but the road from it late Saturday was rockier for Tennesseans than the back trail to Chattanooga.

Wyatt's young men got its first '58 lesson the hard way—from men. Don't bet the Vols won't strike back fighting. They always do.

Defensive First Half

Defense completely dominated offense the first half. Wilson, Wester and the Smith boy named Zeke made life particularly miserable for orange shirts.

The Tigers moved the chains four times but mostly were shackled by superb Tennessee kicking.

Two Majors quick kicks, 62 and 54 yards down the brisk wind, penned the Tigers tightly the first quarter, and when goals were switched, Tennessee kept its hot foot.

The Vols had one major opportunity late in the first period after Lorino popped a punt only 17 yards to the Tiger 35, but Auburn held that line.

The Vols' reserve team was in, Webb directing, and after he completed a six-yard pitch to Don Stephens, two cracks at the riled-up Bengals lost two. Webb then settled a punt on the six.

Vols Help Out

Tennessee finally took the pressure off its foe by a self-inflicted wound, however. A first down snap shot past tailback Webb and when he tracked the ball down, it was 25 yards back on the Vol 13. It was an opportunity for Auburn to saddle up and go—but Tennessee wouldn't hear of it.

Webb got a boot out to the Tennessee 49 but a 15-yard penalty halted Auburn's first hopes. A punt exchange later, Jordan's men started from the Vol 40. Again a penalty came, this for five yards. This was discouraging, too.

Nix finally got a drive engineered in the first half's last two minutes, but it died on the 31.

It had begun at midfield with a nine-yard Nix–Leo Sexton pass. Robbs crunched out the first down on the 38.

Nix ran seven after attempting a pass but three passes went uncaught, one to Lorino, barely high, deep in touchdown land.

Then, Business

Things stayed dull for thousands of goal-line spectators for 10 minutes of the third period. Then business boomed.

Auburn broke out the Oklahoma option series and Tennessee's crashing ends paid the penalty. Nix foxed them out of their boots.

The crushing 67-yard rush took 10 snaps, one play into the fourth period. It was savage to behold.

Robbs and Rawson hammered for seven, then skipped around end, faking, for 22—five of which were deducted for forward lateraling.

Robbs added another yard then Lorino pranced wide to the 26. Nix got three, Robbs six, then dodged on an option toughly down to the five, 12 yards.

Robbs stabbed for one as the quarter ended, then Rawson sailed free for the touchdown, wide left. It was simple running after Nix faked to Robbs, and lobbed to speeding halfback.

Lorino Insures It

Auburn's insurance touchdown was a 43-yarder, in five plays.

The Tiger defense murdered the Vols back 12 yards in three post-kickoff scrimmages, then Lorino darted a 38-yard Majors punt seven yards to the Vol 43.

The Chicago Bears might have stopped the rampaging Tigers but tired, beaten Tennessee wasn't up to it.

Dyas started the parade by stomping nine, then Nix cunningly threw 16 yards to Mike Simmons. Lorino got three, Nix lost nine trying a pass, then Lorino heard another call.

Tommy fielded a high pitch-out streaking right, cut slightly in to worry the defense, then threw it in overdrive. Blocks by Dyas and

Burkett helped, and Lorino dodged into the sideline at the 10, long-gone. It was a big-league run.

Nix's first college try at an extra point was low, and blocked, but no matter, Auburn had 13 points—and defense.

Twice later, Tennessee's downwind kicking set up Vol starts from just outside Auburn's 45, but neither passes, nor runs, nor hopes got any threat generated.

Tennessee's major shot at a first down came in the last minute when little Gene Etter turned end for nine yards.

It was third and one, but a pass attempt ended in a five-yard loss.

Barons Wrap Up Dixie Title (1958)

It's not true, that rumor, said Cal Ermer.

His Southern League playoff and Dixie Series championship Birmingham Barons crowd would not challenge Milwaukee its world belt (assuming the Braves make it—and they will).

"No, sir," the No. 1 field Baron smiled. "We've had it . . . But it's been great while it lasted.

"It was quite a year, quite a gang . . . Yes, I'll have to admit it now. This was the best team I've ever handled."

Ermer spoke in a late Sunday night dressing room, not exactly marked by Sabbatical silence. There were few introverts on the Baron squad which went all the way. When they won a game, they gave forth the good cheer, the rah-rah, razz-ma-taz—and they had just won two.

The Corpus Christi finisher of the best-of-seven series had been Bob Bruce's two-hit, 2–0 shutout. Bill Harrington's four-hitter in the afternoon had draped the Giants on the ropes, 8–3.

Birmingham's fifth Dixie Series triumph had thus come brilliantly in, four games to two. And a season begun with such rosy hopes back in an Ocala, Fla., March, had ended happily after a golden Birmingham October day.

The Barons stuck with a battered, popular victory script to the end.

They teased an afternoon crowd of 1,440 for six innings, dropping behind 3–1, then breaking forth the long ball to come roaring home late.

Howie Phillips and Lou Limmer homers knotted it for Harrington in the sixth . . . and a Gail Henley double, a two-run Steve Demeter two-bagger, and Limmer's second successive roundtripper (also a two-tally shot) had locked the Giants out in a five-run seventh.

Then, after dark, in Rickwood's first Sunday night baseball card ever, Bruce showed the 766 audience the real major league arm he owns.

The big, tackle-looking 25-year-old righthander fanned 13 Texans, and denied third base to them. He didn't slight any of the lineup with his third-strike fastball or curve. He whiffed 'em all.

Bruce walked eight but with his stuff, that didn't frighten his cheerers. Dick Means and Joe Macko reached the big guy for the only Giants hits.

Harrington set his pitching buddy a good example. The Giants used three of their four safeties in run-making—including a two-run Al Stieglitz homer in the second—but the last 15 of them went down in a row to the Little Man's fastballs, curves and knucklers.

It was the 23rd happy verdict of a big comeback year for the 29-year-old ex–big leaguer headed that way again. It marked a 16th straight time for Harrington to pitch in a winning Baron game (24 for 26 since July 9).

Bill's comrades fell calmly before Dick Malbauer for five innings, shocked him with those homers in the sixth, then bombed him out in the seventh. Tommy Bowers and Dick Svode finished.

Knuckler Eddie Fisher was Bruce's victim. He deserved a better four-hit fate.

2
Interlude: Vietnam, 1966

Van Hoose called his Vietnam excursion, in which he followed the U.S. Army's First Division (AKA The Big Red One) the favorite assignment of his career. It was certainly the most important.

For the three months in early 1966 he and photographer Tony Falletta were in Southeast Asia, Van Hoose sent back daily dispatches on the progress of the war, the climate and people of Vietnam and described the horrors of combat as only an experienced soldier could.

Van Hoose and Falletta left for Vietnam just days after Van Hoose had covered Alabama's Orange Bowl victory over Nebraska, which gave the Crimson Tide its third national championship under Paul "Bear" Bryant. It would not take long for Van Hoose to readjust to the rigors of military life.

There are three stories included here, as well as samples of Van Hoose's daily "Vietnam Journal." The first is his opening story in the series, actually written before he left Birmingham. In it, he details his plans for his war correspondence and once and for all draws a line between sports and the "real game" of life.

Also included is a story about the funeral of four men killed in action, in which he movingly includes the text of a poem written by one of the deceased, a poem that was to be published in the next edition of *Stars and Stripes*, the newspaper for active servicemen.

The last of the three major stories is perhaps the most memorable of the Vietnam pieces, Van Hoose's stream-of-consciousness log of any and every thought that might cross a soldier's mind during the quiet hours before battle. This piece, as well as the Vietnam Journal that follows, offers a glimpse of the developing Van Hoose style, a series of rapid-fire ideas and questions asked to oneself (and then answered).

—C.S.

For Now . . . It's a Bigger Game

"I know why you're going to Vietnam," an old friend came at me last week. "Now that you've finished the best story of your career, Alabama winning its third national championship, the hard way, anything else you did in sports would be anti-climactic, strictly Dullsville."

There seemed little point in arguing the matter. The comrade had made up his mind, settled comfortably behind a logical theory, and that was that. Experience had taught that he was a fellow who'd debate his views warmly, at great length, and since there was another shot-taking date due with Dr. Price Edwards—cholera, plague, yellow fever and typhus inoculation scheduled this day—no rebuttal was offered.

But old friend wasn't close to truth, on at least three counts.

Though admitted that Paul Bryant's dramatic jockeying of a talented and dedicated Crimson Tide to another U.S. football championship was quite a story, from November on, it wouldn't rate No. 1 thrill in my book—though it'd be in the top five.

I really don't know which story would rank highest in an 18-year-old pro-spectatoring book. Maybe it would be the Butts libel suit and verdict. It'd be hard to top, anyway.

But I do know that sports will never become flat and stale for me—though I try to remember that games aren't the most important thing in the world—and, I do know that my going to Vietnam isn't an attempt to forsake an old beat.

The flattering assignment to a faraway green spot on a map was accepted because the editorial triumvirate of this big-league paper, Victor Hanson II, Vincent Townsend and John Bloomer, asked me if I wanted it.

Wanted it? I'd walk there to get it if need be.

Why, you ask? Is there football in Saigon? Golf in Pleiku? Baseball in Soc Trang?

No, sir. I hope not.

What I hope is there is an American GI and officer, smarter, tougher, meaner than their dads in another challenge of American arms 20 years ago. I suspect I'll find them there.

So, now it's off to Dallas, San Francisco, Wake, Guam, Manila and Saigon.

And a look-up notebook is filling with names of friends or relatives of friends, Capt. Ralph E. Adams Jr., Tom Stinson, Col. Joe (Bull) Fisher, the Reverend James Livingston, Lt. Walter Copeland, Maj. John King, Capt. Frank Bullock, on and on.

They are there doing a dirty, hazardous, most-time thankless job, and surely they'll appreciate direct word from home.

They'll get that cheering word.

And this man leaving with the colorful Anthony Falletta has had all sorts of cheering words passed to him as he started a countdown toward Monday's Delta Flight 617. All have been appreciated.

Cake, Letters and Dinner

Mrs. Rose Reaves baked a cake, and when this unexcelled cook cooks, one gets the best eating forthwith this side of the Starlight Roof, Waldorf-Astoria Hotel, New York City.

Herb Sadler had a small going-away gift, too, as did Gen. William A. Cunningham of the Fourth Corps, once chief of staff of the Big Red One.

Notes came in profusion, as did telephone calls from Albert Belcher, Jeff Beard, Dan Clark of Lanett, George T. Jones of Monroeville,

Walter S. Houseal of Montgomery, Clarence Roberts, Carl Upchurch of Cuba, Bob Gunn of Jasper, and Judge Whit Windham to name a few.

There was a special letter, too, from the Rev. Ed Kimbrough, which goes in the family Bible because of more than one reason, one of which being that that is an appropriate place to put a message from a distinguished clergyman.

It was a frantic week, last week, all week, but a memorable one.

Certainly, most gracious and happily surprising, was the nice dinner hosted by Mr. and Mrs. Ronald Weathers for it included a family circle as close as any I know in any profession. I could go on, but no need. The point should be established. On with the show.

Big story over? Not a chance. The big challenge is just beginning.

—Sunday, Jan. 16, 1966

Death Seemed Out of Place: Lai Khe, Vietnam, Feb. 3

War brings victory and defeat, life and death. This was death.

There were four empty helmets, graphically, perfectly aligned on the simple table with plain blue cloth and a white cross.

"I am the resurrection and the life," began Chaplain Archie T. Roberts of Stephenson, Mich. "We are gathered today to pay final tribute to four of our comrades . . ."

Death seemed so out of place here, so totally foreign to one of the loveliest places of worship in the world. This was a glorious place to live, to write music, to love.

This was a church, without walls, but a church, without a formal sanctuary, or organ, or cushioned pews—but, still a church.

It was the open-air worship spot that chaplains of the Second Battalion, 28th Infantry, First Division had improvised under the shade of rubber trees now beginning to take on all the gorgeous hues of a North Alabama October.

This was the revered piece of ground where Lt. Col. George S. Eyster Jr., S-Sgt. Joe Correll, PFC Andrew Henry and PFC Richard Tucker had visited occasionally before Operation Crimp.

"I knew all four of our comrades," the young, intense Methodist minister went on. "Each was a man of strong faith.

"Each knew how to face life, and, as a direct result, each knew how to face death.

"We all find it difficult to find words to pay tribute to them, now departed. But I think each of them could say with Paul, 'I have fought the good fight; I have finished the course; I have kept the faith.'"

The Reverend Roberts, his chaplain's cloth around his neck, then prayed, first for the four American soldiers, already flown to final resting spots back home, next for their families, and finally for their comrades, who hope the sword they bear will bring peace to a rich but violated land of war for more than 20 years.

The ceremony, 24 minutes long, attracted three choppers from Big Red One headquarters. Each chopper, carrying five passengers in addition to pilots and gun crew, had a general officer aboard, Maj. Gen. Jonathan O. Seaman, CG, Big Red One and his assistant commanders, Brig. Gen. Randolph C. Dickens and Brig. Gen. Charles M. Mount.

The demands of war do not afford many senior officers the time to recognize death in the ranks, but Big Red leaders find time.

This proud, tradition-loving division is a family, and ties are tight, from top to bottom.

Lt. Col. Eyster was reared to be a soldier and that he was. His father is a general, and the son would have been one also but last week you might have read what happened.

Peter Arnett wrote it for Associated Press, for he was near the battalion commander when he was hit once by a Viet Cong sniper, then hit again.

Except for a valorous helicopter pilot, Col. Eyster might not have survived the jungle trail. But the pilot ignored ground fire, picked up Col. Eyster, and evacuated him. He looked as if he'd make it then. But a blood clot formed, and it took him away, swiftly, two days later.

The enlisted men honored with Col. Eyster went quickly, also, either by sniper fire or booby trap.

For Tucker, of Charlie Company, death cheated him of his big moment. Like a number of soldiers, lonesome and dreaming, Tucker whiled away foxhole time writing poetry. His buddies told him it was good stuff.

So, Tucker sent one of his poems to *Stars and Stripes*, the worldwide newspaper of the American armed services. It went like this and *Stars and Stripes* editors liked it, too. They accepted it:

Oh lonely soldier all alone,
    You know why you're away from home.
There's a job to be done, a war to be won
    You know you're not here just for fun.
You go out on a sweep through the day.
    But before you leave, you stop to pray.
That God will follow you, wherever you go,
    To protect and guide you, when you meet the foe.
You're out there sweating in the long day's heat,
    And when you return you're really beat.
But before you retire you stop and pray:
    "Thank you, Lord, for letting me live another day."

The edition carrying Tucker's poem was en route to the combat zone when Tucker was killed. He never saw it in print.

              —Friday, Feb. 4, 1966

A GI's Thoughts before Battle:
Michelin Plantation, Vietnam, Feb. 28

Twenty-odd years it's been, but all has not been forgotten.

    Attack time minus thirty, and you're shivering. Something about weather anywhere, just before dawn. You think it's chilling, even nest-ling the equator.

Gosh, aren't the stars pretty. Were they ever brighter, even on those clear, cold December nights with W. E. Mitchell in Toomsuba Creek swamp, hunting possums?

Yeah, there she is, the Big Dipper. Sitting a lot lower in the sky than back home. And there's the North Star. Can North be thataway?

Army hasn't changed a bit. Get you up an hour early, then make you wait.

That was good coffee this morning. Always is, just before you jump off—just like it is when you have your next one, knowing you haven't been hit.

Those kids lying quietly all around. Bravo Company, 2nd Infantry, Big Red One. They're so young—babies. Were we this young?

Wonder what they're thinking, inside that pot helmet, steel, exactly like we had . . . Could one guess? . . . One could, if he's been in their boots. But no one else:

Good coffee this morning, for a change. Wonder what Alvarez put in it, though? Just went 10 minutes ago. Gotta go again now. Same thing happened on the first day of that last operation.

We sure are unlucky . . . Charlie Company's reserve again today. Last time it was Able. Bravo always has to be the point. Ever'body says it's because we take our objective. Those other guys aren't worth a damn. We're always bailing them out of trouble.

Damn it, who was that wise guy over there who said "this is it." Prob-ably that new guy in from Benning. He's seen too many movies . . . Ain't that a laugh? Saw a guy slip up on a Jap tank the other night in one, blow it all to pieces with a grenade. What a joke—but civilians don't know any better. I bet they thought it was hot stuff.

Folks back in the States don't know nothing about war. And don't care. Don't even know a war's going on.

If I get hit today, hope it's a light one, through the leg. Sgt. Sini got it the other day, right below the knee. Didn't touch a bone. He's probably back in the States now, out of this hellhole.

Johnson's back there, too. Took some shrapnel in his shoulder. Our own stuff. If we were as careless as our artillery, they'd court-martial us. They just shoot.

I'm gonna shoot today, too, at anything that moves. I've been awful lucky . . . Claymore got Martin and Cheney right next to me last week. Don't see how it missed me.

Bullet gotta have your name on it——I know that. But there ain't many of us old 2nd men left. These new guys are good kids, but they don't know what they're doing.

Damn, listen at that. Those 52s really shake old Charlie. How can he live through that? Listen! . . . I couldn't take that and stick in those tunnels, but he can.

How does he live on that rice . . . and dig all those tunnels? He's a tough one, smart too. He ain't about to stand up and fight us, man-to-man. We'd murder him.

He don't let you see him, either. We'd murder him. He'll leave some old guys behind, a slant-eye or two, and he'll shoot and run.

If you ask me all these people are VC. How come these ARVN guys aren't fighting? They know we'll do it for them, that's why.

Damn, that coffee was strong. But it was good. I wonder if I got up and went again, Marv would think I was nervous?

Lot of guts, that guy. I saw him walk right up to that bunker the other morning. Lotta guts.

Wonder if they gonna get our mail to us today? Didn't hear from Frances yesterday. She usually writes every day.

She's a fine gal. I didn't know she felt that way before I left. Fine gal, lot to her. Man's a fool to mess around with other women when there's a gal like that. I'm gonna quit it.

I'm going to church more when I get back, too——if I get back. I know I ought to, but something was always coming up.

Hey there, I hear choppers. They're something, those choppers. They put you right there. Those pilots have guts.

"Yes, sir, we're ready, Lieutenant. My squad's in the second chopper, and we go right when hit. Yes, sir, we're all set.

"Okay, you guys, shake it. We're in No. 2. Don't get itchy fingers when you're down. You might need it later.

"We missed old Charlie last time. Let's git him."

—Wednesday, March 1, 1966

Vietnam Journal, January 23, 1966

First impressions of Vietnam, from land and air:

Beautiful country from 2,000 feet up. Marvelous mixture of greens below, pale, dark, chartreuse, yellowish, bluish . . . Terrain remindful of Florida just below Miami, sandy-looking soil, murky river bottom, shady forest . . . Roads are red clayish, ribbons of dust. Villages are spaced patternless along road, mostly from 20 to 50 houses.

Jeep's eye view of same territory reveals incredible filth . . . Mention this fact to Far East veteran and it immediately gets a response: "If you think this is bad, you ought to go see Korea" (or India, or Formosa, or Burma).

The hordes of small children interesting. Many of them are learning GI language fast. First English: "Chew gum, please?"

Twentieth Century transportation is all mixed up with 2,000 BC— jeep and powerful trucks with ox carts, the half-mile per hour kind. American drivers have Rule No. 1: The right-of-way belongs to South Vietnamese.

~

Strategic view of Vietnamese War after preliminary questions to several combat experts (none of whom can be quoted, directly):

Anybody predicting a definitive victory in this thing (particularly an early conquest date) is naïve. No one really familiar with factors involved, political and military, will guess ultimate V-VN Day.

One particularly brilliant observer did say that we won't now lose this war. But, he added, if we'd waited one month longer to start our buildup here, we probably could have stayed home.

Simply stated, the situation now is that we control the area housing most of the South Vietnam population of at least 15 million. Viet Cong control 70 per cent of the land area.

South Vietnam faintly resembles Florida. Climate is akin, too, and size. SVN has roughly 65,000 square miles, about 20 percent larger than Alabama.

Saigon population is at least 2 million, squeezed into an area only 30 square miles (not nearly as large as Birmingham). It's an inland port, some 50 miles from the China Sea on Saigon River. A tour of dock area reminds one of Mobile, only it's at least 1,000 per cent dirtier, and shaggier looking. Had Viet Cong ever taken over Saigon, one military spokesman says, the war would have been over right then.

First division combat area, the hottest in the war, comprises some 10,000 square miles. Big Red One defends key spots. Ground outside defensive perimeter belongs to VC.

Viet Cong assiduously seek opportunity for equal-size fight with South Vietnamese army but, after painful experience, do not jump American forces one-third its manpower.

January 25: Early Reflections on the Viet Cong Soldier

The fellow who may have pulled the world off the brink and to an un-wanted third world war in 50 years is first of all a scrawny, runty chap, the type American he-man would slap in an argument, not fist-fight. From five to five and a half feet tall, he usually runs from 100 to 120 pounds.

He's all muscle and bone, however, like a horse jockey, and he's ag-ile. Since illiteracy in this land runs to 80 per cent, chances are 4–1 he's lacking in formal schooling. But he's American pioneer—smart in sur-vival techniques and he makes worldwide laws of nature work for him, to his advantage.

He concedes the American, and his enemy fellow countrymen, the day. He rules the night.

Americans who fought Japanese in Guadalcanal and New Guinea, in the Philippines and Okinawa, grudgingly consider the Viet Cong a tougher adversary, though not nearly as dangerously equipped. The VC are more ingenious with their weapons than the Japanese, and, above all, more patient.

They are workers, too, as miles of tunnels which mark their defensive strongholds attest. Every hole they've dug cost the digger a bucket of sweat and energy, for pick and shovel labor in this Alabama-type August heat and humidity is brutal drudgery.

His courage is unquestioned. He will be taken prisoner but seldom with a gun in his hands. Somebody has taught him fanaticism, and discipline. These traits mark his combat deportment.

He retreats from all equal challenges—unless one of his base camps is threatened—and, apparently, he's content to make time work for him. Chances are he's been fighting all his adult life, against the Japanese, French, South Vietnamese or Americans, and he's resigned to 10, 20 or 30 more years of it, if need be.

He subsists on rice and salt but he'll take anything better from a noncombatant if he figures he can.

They say he's a creature of habit and superstition, and this has hurt him—and will hurt him more, perhaps fatally. His tactics are simple, geared to his intelligence level, and until five months ago they were proving effective enough to win a war.

The time which he thought was his might be running in the other direction now, as Americans now pour into the ring against him in powerful and increasing legions. His rifle will now be trumped by long range gun and rocket.

Still, he's ever dangerous yet, and he'll adapt to conditions-to-be with cunning and skill.

He's a man to study fuller. More later.

January 27

Letters to Moms and Pops Back Home

Don't you hate a tattletale? Hate me. I'm going to peach on your boy over here.

First thing you notice here is that his color taste runs to green: green uniform (though dusty), green cap, green equipment, canteen, belt, rifle and radio. Underwear's green, too. Army made him dye it.

Next thing catches you quickly is his size, particularly compared to other people who walk foreign streets and paths. Natives remain amazed they grow 'em so big in America.

This Joe is bigger than you were, Dad, taller and huskier. Smarter, too. Read somewhere that 75 per cent of 1965 Army were high school grads, compared with 48 per cent in Korean War era.

His language is no more colorful than yours in World War II, Pop, nor more diversified. Old terms remain, probably some dating back to Hannibal.

This kid probably adapts, psychologically anyway, to extreme temperature better than an older generation did in South Pacific. At least a tourist doesn't hear constant complaining heard 20 years back.

This fellow here lives in energy-sapping heat, amid snakes, bugs, flies, ants and dust—always that dust until it's mud—and though he doesn't enjoy it, he doesn't continually gripe.

And they say mud here is true knee-deep type. Back home, you know, when mud gets low-cut shoe depth, it immediately is referred to as "knee-deep."

No complaints much about chow, either, not persistent type that is. There really shouldn't have been 20, 25 years ago. Food for most soldiers, now as then, is better than they get by home firesides.

Menu here, as anywhere, is as excellent as its cook. In last two decades, however, a sensitive army has devoted a campaign to better train its cooks and bakers.

Maybe because of superior education, Dad, son is a more disciplined soldier than were you. The kid is more philosophical. He doesn't rent fatigue clothes, build wailing walls, bemoaning his foreign travel.

This GI takes better care of himself, healthwise, than you did, Mr. Daddy. He's better taught to do so.

In short, and more on this later, this American is not an ugly American at all. You should be proud of him—and doubtless you are.

Van Hoose in Central Park, New York, 1940. Courtesy Van Hoose family.

A 21-year-old Alf Van Hoose, left, with brother Jim and sister, Mary Owen, 1941. Courtesy Van Hoose family.

Van Hoose in Europe, 1945. Courtesy
Van Hoose family.

Van Hoose with son, Alf III, left, and
daughter, Susanna, 1950s. Courtesy
Van Hoose family.

In *The Birmingham News* sports office with Benny Marshall, 1953.
Courtesy Van Hoose family.

Getting a lucky rabbit's foot from daughter Susanna upon departing for
Vietnam, January 1966. Courtesy Van Hoose family.

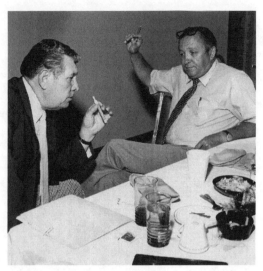

Van Hoose, right, enjoys an after-dinner cigar with Coach Ralph "Shug" Jordan, early 1970s. Courtesy Van Hoose family.

"Burr" with his favorite fan, grandson Gil Rogers, 1979. Courtesy Van Hoose family.

On the golf course with Coach Paul "Bear" Bryant,
late 1970s. Courtesy Van Hoose family.

Van Hoose's *Birmingham News* mug-
shot, late 1980s. Courtesy Van Hoose
family

3
Glory Days, 1959–1983

Van Hoose's rise as a regular columnist at *The News* dovetails nicely with the re-emergence of Alabama football under Paul "Bear" Bryant. Although Auburn and other state schools certainly got their due, many of the top stories in the prime of Van Hoose's career would involve the Crimson Tide.

Columns detailing memorable Alabama wins—1971 Southern Cal, 1979 Penn State—and losses—1972 Auburn, 1980 Mississippi State—are included here, as much for their significance as their style (although the 1980 MSU piece contains one of Van Hoose's finest lead paragraphs). Also in this chapter is Van Hoose's game column on the 1982 Iron Bowl, Auburn's first victory over Alabama in 10 years.

Reprinted here are several columns regarding Bryant—his record-tying 314th win in 1981, his retirement in 1982, his death six weeks later. Bryant was a singular figure in athletics in this state, and no one in the media knew him better than Van Hoose.

Van Hoose also helped stoke a rivalry between Birmingham and Atlanta that exists to this day with his coverage of the *Saturday Evening Post* lawsuits. Furman Bisher, longtime sports editor of the *Atlanta Journal-Constitution* (who is, in fact, still on staff at the *AJC*) wrote a story for the *Saturday Evening Post* in 1961 in which he focused on brutality in college football, naming Bryant as Public Enemy No. 1.

Bryant subsequently sued for that article, and a more famous one published the following year that implicated Bryant and former Georgia coach Wally Butts in a plot to fix the outcome of the 1962 Bama-Georgia game (won 35–0 by Alabama). Van Hoose called the trial, which eventually ended in a massive jury award to Butts and a six-figure settlement to Bryant and shattered the already creaky credibility of *The Post,* the top sports assignment of his career. Two articles on the trial, one centering on Bryant's captivating testimony and the other focusing on the aftermath, are reprinted here.

There are also two special columns reprinted here, one written after the death of Van Hoose's friend and mentor Benny Marshall, who committed suicide in 1969. For someone who was in the business as long as he was, Van Hoose had the unfortunate task of eulogizing many friends and acquaintances, but never as movingly as he did in the case of Marshall.

Then there is a column written on the eve of his daughter's wedding in 1975. Therein, Van Hoose revels in the joy and pride of fatherhood, while also lamenting the events and occasions his job required him to miss.

Also worth mentioning is what has to be among Van Hoose's finest columns of all, a 1965 piece about an otherwise non-noteworthy celebrity golf tournament in Monroeville. Van Hoose effectively twists every rule of style, using first-person, second-person and third-person voice to relate a conversation with star football player Lance Alworth to an on-site observer and then to thousands of his readers.

Then there are a few "special event" columns—including the one he wrote in 1974 after Hank Aaron of the Atlanta Braves surpassed Babe Ruth as baseball's home run king. Not included here is a second-day comment about the same event, in which Van Hoose wryly observed the crowd at Atlanta Stadium, diminished from 55,775 to 10,648 the night after Aaron's historic clout, as similar to one at church the Sunday after Easter.

The death of Bryant was really chosen as an arbitrary end to this stage of Van Hoose's career, but the coach's passing was most certainly the end of an era in Alabama. Coverage of statewide sports had changed overnight.

—C.S.

"No Sir!" Tide's Bryant Answers Rigging Accusations (August 8, 1963)

Atlanta—"No sir!" resounded again and again in Federal Court here today on the most dramatic morning of the dramatic four-day-old $10 million Wallace Butts vs. Curtis Publishing Co. libel suit.

And the "No sir!" man was Paul (Bear) Bryant.

Several times he said it softly, sometimes with a smile, occasionally darkly, and at the finish his tone was belligerent.

The Alabama coach and athletic director played the scale in one hour and 51 minutes of testifying.

"NO SIR!" he told Butts' attorney, William H. Schroder, in an hour of direct testimony, he would not have paid any attention to any information from Georgia athletic director Butts or anybody at Georgia, before last September's football game, which *The Post* said was "rigged" and "fixed."

"If he had given me anything," Bryant said, "I wouldn't have used it. He's for Georgia. I'm for Alabama and I'm trying to beat him."

"No sir!" Bryant fairly shouted at Curtis lawyer Welborn Cody during his surprisingly short 12 minutes of cross-examining.

The letter that University of Alabama President Frank A. Rose sent Georgia President O. C. Aderhold didn't admit Bryant and Butts talked about specific formations in two lengthy telephone conversations several days prior to the game.

"And when Dr. Rose gets in this (witness) chair," Bryant all but yelled, "he'll explain what he meant."

"No sir," Bryant answered in various tones as Schroder went through the famous notes supposedly taken down by Atlanta insuranceman George Burnett. He (Bryant) wasn't exactly sure what this or that meant, football-wise.

Bryant denied most of Burnett's notes after reading each one, point-by-point, through Butts' glasses.

When handed the notes, which Curtis had placed on exhibit, Bryant said he'd have to borrow some glasses to read along as Schroder quizzed him.

He had evidently mislaid his on the plane coming over last night, Bryant said.

Three members of the jury quickly offered Bryant their specs but after trying on two pair of them and finding they didn't help, Schroder brought up Butts' glasses and Bryant said he could see through them.

The incident was one of several which humorously lightened a tension-heavy morning.

Bryant also brought some titters from the packed audience in Judge Lewis Morgan's courtroom with some colorful, backwoodsy answers to highly technical football questions.

At one time, Bryant labeled a particular defensive movement as "gobble-wobble."

In answering a query about a Burnett note, which said that Georgia safetyman Brigham Woodward committed himself fast, Bryant said, "If we'd a-known that, and didn't throw at his area, I oughtta been bored for the hollow head. And we didn't throw a pass at him all night."

In answering another Burnett note about a quarterback who'd run if the defensive man was blocked and pass if he wasn't, Bryant said, "That was really funny."

"If my little boy didn't run with the ball after somebody blocked his way open, I'd spank him," Bryant said.

Bryant said that if he and Butts had "rigged" the game then, "We ought to go to jail."

Alabama's coach said that "There might have been a couple of things (in Burnett's notes) that I would rather have known than not know. But the kinds of things I'd like to know were not in the notes."

Bryant said that he and Butts had talked a lot about "football in general" and rules interpretations.

He said both had investments in an organization known as Continental Enterprises and had lost heavily. He said that he had not been talked into the investment by Butts.

Bryant, a surprise leadoff man as the presentation of Butts' case began, was followed in the stand by Jimmy Sharpe of Montgomery, a guard on the 1962 team.

Sharpe said, among other things, that Georgia had used one formation which "confused" the Alabama defense and that Alabama had to alter its defensive tactics.

Charley Pell, a tackle from Albertville who also participated in the game (Sept. 22, 1962) at Legion Field in Birmingham, was scheduled to testify this afternoon.

Butts sat at a counsel table and appeared to be listening attentively.

Bryant was asked if he recalled a telephone conversation of last Sept. 13—the date on which *The Post* said Butts gave the Alabama coach detailed information about Georgia's team.

"I don't know whether he made the call or not. According to records I've seen he did," he said.

Q: "Have you any recollection of what was said?"
A: "Specifically, no sir."
Q: "On Sunday, Sept. 16, 1962, *The Post* said, you and Coach Wallace Butts had another telephone conversation?"
A: "I'm familiar with it (the article), but I do not remember whether or not I made the call. But again, according to the telephone records, I made the call."

Bryant identified diagrams made on a chalkboard by Georgia Coach Johnny Griffith, as commonly used slot formations. He was asked if

Georgia employed the formations in its 1962 spring football game scouted by Alabama.

"They certainly did."

He was asked about Alabama's scouting report on that game.

"According to our reports, the slot was used by Georgia 109 times in the spring game," Bryant said.

Bryant said he did not make any significant changes in defensive plans between Sept. 13 and the game nine days later.

The Post closed its defense in Butts' $10 million libel suit with surprising suddenness Wednesday afternoon.

Immediately, Butts' attorneys moved for a directed verdict.

U.S. District Judge Lewis R. Morgan denied it, but with the jury ushered from the crowded courtroom, he told the lawyers:

"I'm going to charge the jury that the article is libelous per se," and that Curtis Publishing Co. (publisher of *The Post*), "has the burden of proving the sting of the libel was true and it is up to the jury to decide."

Judge Morgan told Butts' lawyers, denying their motion for a directed verdict, that "I think you'd be jeopardizing your whole case to take it from the jury."

Allen Lockerman, one of Butts' lawyers, had told the judge, "We felt we should make a motion for direction by the court. We do feel the defendant has not proved the truth under the burden he has."

Lockerman said that the magazine had charged Butts with being a "fixer," a "rigger," with having fixed and rigged a game in 1962 by furnishing all the vital secrets and information concerning Georgia's plays, both offense and defense, to Coach Bryant.

"Under the plea of justification *The Post* had the burden of proving by a preponderance of evidence under the law that those things are true.

"They have not proved them," Lockerman said.

Butts' presentations began with reading of a deposition from Frank Graham Jr., the freelance writer whose name appeared on the article in the March 23 issue of the magazine.

Graham's deposition said, in part, that he had never seen the notes Atlanta insuranceman George Burnett said he took while eavesdropping on a Bryant-Butts conversation.

Graham said that he had met with Furman Bisher (*Atlanta Journal* sports editor) in New York when Bisher had come to offer a story about Georgia football to *The Post*.

The Post already had the information, Graham said, but it was agreed Bisher would go back to Atlanta and research added material for the article.

Graham said that Roderick Beddow, defending *The Post* in an earlier libel action filed by Bryant, had sent the magazine the information which initiated the article.

Graham told of a meeting in Atlanta with Beddow; the late Fred Bodeker, a private investigator; Pierre Howard, an attorney; and Milton Flack, a friend of Burnett's at which they discussed payment for the story.

Representing *The Post*, Graham made an offer to pay $2,000 to Burnett, but both Flack and Howard thought the price should be higher.

Graham entered into an agreement, he said, to pay $2,000 for Burnett's affidavit concerning the telephone conversation, and $3,000 additionally if *The Post* published the story exclusively.

Asked where Bisher had obtained the information with which he first approached *The Post*, Graham said, "Apparently he got a good bit of it from Cook Barwick."

Barwick is a member of the Georgia athletic board, and an attorney. He has been in the courtroom as an observer since trial of the suit began Monday.

Graham said that, never having seen Burnett's notes, he depended upon "the recollections" of Flack and Howard as to what Burnett had told them.

He said he interviewed no one in connection with the article except Flack, Burnett, Howard and Bisher, and that he had sent Bisher a copy of the article early in March, approximately two weeks before its publication.

Wednesday's testimony opened with Johnny Griffith, the Georgia coach, making a surprise return to the stand.

Griffith testified that he had first heard from Bob Edwards—Burnett's intermediary—in connection with the charges against Butts "sometime before Christmas, 1962."

The magazine wrote and Burnett testified Tuesday that he first informed Edwards of his note-taking on Jan. 4.

Griffith was asked by Schroder if his testimony was that the only thing of benefit in what Burnett said he heard concerned two Georgia formations?

Griffith said, "Yes."

Frank Inman, a member of Griffith's staff last season, testified that the information Burnett said he heard Butts passing to Bryant last Sept. 12 could have helped Alabama in its preparation for the game.

Inman was followed to the stand by Leroy Pearce, another Georgia assistant coach. He said the notes which have been handed from witness to witness until they're becoming worn "concerned the offense of the team being talked about."

—August 8, 1963

Bryant to Butts: "What Happened to Rest of It?" (August 21, 1963)

Atlanta—F. M. Williams, one of the real pros of our profession, wrote the finest story he's ever done here Tuesday. It lasted two paragraphs.

"Paul Bryant made another telephone call to Wally Butts today," wrote Williams.

"Hey, Wally," said Bryant. "What happened to the rest of it?"

It was that kind of a day, however, a day to bring out the best in many people.

There was Wally Butts, back from the walking dead again, king of the earth's little men again, prince of the meek once more, the people who'll inherit the earth.

Wally had just inherited a goodly portion of the earth's goods, and was attempting, not very successfully, to wear the mask.

"How do you feel," asked one fellow who'll never see $3,000,000 in his whole life.

"Very humble," replied Butts—and he wasn't play-acting this time.

It was the kind of day which sent a desperately weary, amazingly sleepless Wally Butts over to shake the hand of a man who kept applying the whip last week with two relentless questions: "What about this man's character? . . . Would you believe him under oath?"

He Knew the Answers

Curtis counselor Welborn Cody had known the answers beforehand of each distinguished Georgia educator to whom he asked it, but he went right on.

And Butts walked over and shook hands with his adversary, turned his cheek so to speak, like the good book advises.

This was before a dead-pan jury filed in, mind you, to start wires humming round the world.

Ah yes, this had to been one of those half dozen really memorable days a man is lucky to actually live.

That pause as a clerk of court read "we the jury" has to rate unforgettable.

It has to rate with an unseen man named John Glenn, sitting above hellish fire on a TV screen, about to fly where angels fly, and Col. Shorty Powers dramatically counting down: six . . . five . . . four . . . three . . . two . . . one.

It was that moment in Pittsburgh, late on a gorgeous and glorious October afternoon in '60, and Bill Mazeroski lashing a Ralph Terry pitch from Forbes Field.

This was that supreme moment re-created, when Douglas A. MacArthur was laying down his sword in the hallowed hall of the U.S. Congress.

"Old soldiers never die."

This was living . . . and this man knew it.

This was personal vindication in a newspaperman—this one a newspaperman conscious of the loftiest traditions of our profession, trying to be objective as this historic drama unfolded, but knowing he couldn't be.

Objective? How?

How could a man remain objective, unfeeling, as fact after fact rolled up to show how cruelly devastating the pen can be if unchecked by basic ethics?

It was a scene of humans acting like humans, tears of joy and tension from he-men and their women.

One could recall the man Butts a few days before, so awfully alone it seemed, talking almost to himself.

"I'm no angel, I've made mistakes and I'm sorry. But this? I'm telling the truth."

His was a day to remember . . . and I remember.

Namath Has Booster: Superstar Alworth (1965)

A lady watching tee-off time in the Monroeville Invitational Thursday had an inquiry of a pencil-and-notebook man:

SHE: Who was that boy you were talking to?
HE (remembering old vaudeville patter): That wasn't a boy. That was a man—one of pro football's superstars.
SHE: G'wan with you. No jokes please. That young boy? He's gotta be still in high school, and, besides, he isn't big enough for pro football. Also, he's too nice-looking.
SHE (after a stage pause, triumphantly clinching her case): On top of that, what would he be doing in Monroeville?

HE (triumphantly, too): Well, you've brought up several points, interesting points. And if you'll sit quietly, you'll get a preview of a Sunday column in *The Birmingham News*.

And . . . this is what she heard.

"That muscular young fellow is Lance Alworth, now of Little Rock. During the fall, he's a flankerback with the San Diego Chargers, one of the half-dozen men in his league (the American Football League) the other crowd (National Football League) grudgingly admits could star in its ranks.

"I just talked to Lance about that NFL sentiment and he grinned a good grin. Said he didn't care to get into any fussing match but that the Chargers would be willing to take on the Cleveland Browns, Baltimore Colts, Green Bay Packers or any team on a winner-take-all basis.

"He added that he thought the Charger defensive front was the best in football."

Fracchia the Finest

The lady didn't raise her hand but it could be sensed she had a question ready. She had one. And she asked it.

Was this young man in the same league that Joe Namath was?

"Yes," he replied, "at least Namath is headed for that league."

And I joshed Alworth about Namath, too, asking if he was envious of all that money Joe got.

He said he wasn't, that Joe getting that kind of dough would help everybody, raise the salary standard all down the line.

Alworth also said that Namath had come into the AFL "at the right time, with the right talent and the right position."

He said he was "all for Namath" and he believed if Joe went to the Jets camp with the right attitude, and he had ability, that his teammates wouldn't be a bit jealous, either.

Alworth also said he had great respect for Alabama football players. He met 'em "only once," he said (in the Tide's 10–3 '62 Sugar Bowl conquest of Arkansas), and he admired the vigorous manner they played the game.

He also admired the running ability of Mike Fracchia that afternoon. Best back he ever played against, anywhere. Alworth went on, "what a shame he got that knee hurt and couldn't make it back."

Kiwanis Club Date

Now, as to what Alworth's doing in Monroeville, well, first he's playing in a golf tournament. That's Walter Wood of Birmingham, Downing Gray of Pensacola, and Forest Watkins of Monroeville with him.

One of that foursome should win this thing (and Gray did).

Secondly, Alworth is here to speak at the Kiwanis Club's Ladies Night function. His wife's uncle got him to come. He's the Rev. Reed Polk, pastor of the First Baptist Church, Monroeville.

Lance said he wasn't a full-time worker for that fine Fellowship of Christian Athletes society, but that he was all for it, and tried to accept all the church-related projects he could.

Also Liked Golf

He said he also liked golf, though his advertising business in Little Rock dulled his golf swing.

When he got to play much, he reported, he could shoot in the mid-70s.

And it was true, Alworth admitted, that he birdied the first three holes of a winter exhibition match in Jackson, Miss., against Mickey Mantle and Joe Fortunado.

It was also true, back at Brookhaven, Miss., High, that he had been a pro baseball prospect. Best offer he'd gotten to sign, and forget football, was $50,000 from the Pittsburgh Pirates.

The New York Yankees had gone to $30,000, Alworth remembered, and had asked to get a later shot at competition.

Alworth had also run dashes at Brookhaven, and also at Arkansas. His best time, he said, was 9.5, twice, though he bettered that in a couple of other meets "with a wind at my back—but that shouldn't count."

He said he was six feet tall, weighed 185, and that Sunday he'd start getting in shape to report to San Diego, July 19. By getting in shape, he said, he meant increased running.

He hadn't regretted favoring football over baseball, he said. He said baseball was too tough, mentally.

Baseball, he put it, gave him too much time to fret if he was going 0-for-4."

"I'm a natural worrier," Alworth said. "But in football I don't worry. I just do things that come natural for me."

—Sunday, May 25, 1965

Tigers Go for KO—And Get It (1965)

Auburn—It wasn't a great Auburn team that licked Florida here Saturday, 28–17. Not in the sense of some several other Ralph Jordan teams, one of which won a national championship.

But for a final 30 minutes, as a homecoming crowd of 45,000 warmed up on a cool October afternoon, Auburn never had a bunch of Tigers who played farther beyond normal abilities.

Florida had blanked Auburn without a first down for 28 minutes, remember?—and Florida had confidently carried a 10–0 edge to halftime rest.

But the Tigers returned to the ring, down but not out, dedicated to the knockdown play or nothing, and what a show this one became.

The Tigers got that knockdown play four times. Three would have been sufficient.

Alex Bowden triggered two of them with his stout right arm—
29 yards to Scotty Long, 69 yards to Freddie Hyatt.

Bill Cody handled the other two, as an All-American line-backer—
tromping one pass interception 29 yards, and curling around a late
fumble for another touchdown which put the deep freeze on Florida
hopes so warm and bright in early afternoon.

But Cody and Bowden, stalwart architects of victory though they
were, deserve only a mite more applause than a score of other Tiger
youngsters.

This was a day of super performance for every Auburn warrior. Each
dedicated himself to get this one in—each deserves commendation.

Coaches, Too

An Auburn coaching staff deserves some credit, too. Football is still, as
always it will be, a game of leadership.

Ralph Jordan spent a week jabbing a psychological needle into a
Florida which had talked itself to greatness again—and also had played
like a great team on occasion, like against Ole Miss.

Jordan also worked a week on Drake Field making shifts here, patch-
ing up a wounded situation there, and never letting his boys forget a
minute they could win themselves a Saturday celebration.

No Auburn team since 1962, headed for Alabama, had been as crippled
for combat. No Auburn team since Jordan got here had been an eight-
point underdog on its home field, either.

But Auburn coaches demanded extra effort nevertheless and Auburn
players reached farther back for confidence and steadfastness, and you
know what resulted.

One of Auburn's most satisfying wins ever, that's what.

Men to Remember

Anybody who saw what happened through the naked eye, or through
the penetrating gaze of the TV camera, should have memories from
this affair.

There was that futile Auburn attack for nearly a half . . . and then Mr. Bowden making a debut.

There was that defense for 60 minutes, sometimes out-finessed, oft-times out-slickered by the awesome talent of Steve Spurrier and Charles Casey, but never out-fought.

There was Tommy Lunceford punting again, high and far, and remember (from linebacker) Marvin Tucker fighting off hordes of wide-blocking Gators, all day.

You should remember Jack Thornton and Bobby Walton pursuing Spurrier, too, like Canadian Mounties, downing him at every opportunity.

You should remember these monster Florida linemen, too, agile and mean, who came to play this day also, and play they did.

This wasn't a little league-type outfit Auburn finally pitched into a pit. These were men, football men, pro-type men.

It was just one of those days which finally turned out to be beautiful for Auburns, after all sort of early perils and pitfalls, plus a 10–0 deficit at halftime.

If anybody says he knew Auburn would win this thing right then—anybody except a coach or player—you can call him a prevaricator . . . The truth ain't in him.

For 30 minutes Auburn looked no part a winner—those first 30 minutes.

But they got there finally, these Tigers got there grandly, and it was something to see.

He Was Just Benny (1969)

Now we'll never know how it really was in a truly little old New York the night the Mets won a championship.

We were going to be told about it, in this space, he had promised, as he slowly drove up Red Mountain Thursday in God's lovely twilight.

He had the column all written in his head, Bennett Davis Marshall twinkled his little boy grin, and he'd get it on paper as soon as he got home, hugged Ruth and the young Marshalls, Ellen and Matt, grabbed a quick nap, and returned to the battered, old typewriter he loved.

Benny Marshall took that last story with him. We know only this. It'd have been a great one, maybe with just a mite of whimsy, certainly full of smiles, and surely he'd touch on the heavenly joy he said he'd just experienced in a big city which too often tries to hide such emotion.

It'd have been a great column because Mr. Marshall couldn't do a bad one. Not if he tried. God endowed him with talent not squandered on ordinary man—and though Benny knew this, he never spoke about it.

Others did, particularly those who knew him best. And not with jealous envy, either. This we considered, might be sacrilege. It would have been.

Now, he's gone.

How do you say goodbye to an old friend?

Who can, really?

Who should really try?

He was here, and he ran his race. He hadn't felt good in the last few weeks, but he masked it well.

Those who worked around him sensed it. Nothing was said.

It was football time, his time of year, and the season was a great, glad time to be alive.

Saturday he'd be in Tuscaloosa, with bands playing, pretty girls stepping, and men exceeding courage right out there in front to entertain him, and you, and his reading public.

And Monday he knew he'd get letters, from people he so wanted to please, fussing that he was anti-Alabama, or anti-Auburn, or anti-somebody.

Benny Marshall was never anti-anyone, or actually, anti-anything. This unnaturalness sometime puzzled him, and occasionally he asked the question, more to himself than to any listener.

"Maybe I should be more that way."

But, he knew he shouldn't be—and he wasn't.

He was Benny Marshall, with an IQ which had his teachers doing double-takes, and double-promoting him by early teenhood into Howard College.

He was Benny Marshall, off to a war foreign to his instincts of live-and-let-live, but an airman ultimately of courage and dedication.

He was Benny Marshall, newspaperman, appreciated fullest only by those who worked with and against him, for scores of little things he did which made his subtle touch, his labor distinctive.

He was Benny Marshall, listener, watcher, worker, above all, worker.

He was the smile that came to this place in mid-morning in recent years—before that, for 20-odd years, the happy face arriving before daylight.

He was Benny Marshall, author, too, and though he could hide occasional personal pressure and gloom, he couldn't bridle his joy at someone's mention of this. He had written two outstanding books. He knew they were outstanding.

He was Benny Marshall, uncommon man, but not in his thinking. He was always modestly centerstage in a crowd, though he pushed others forward.

He was Benny Marshall, friend—and thousands know it.

None will say goodbye.

—Friday, Sept. 26, 1969

Shug Forgot the Holding Bit at 39 (1970)

James Ralph Jordan, who turns 60 today, confesses he's blown it badly on the matter of birthdays.

For one thing, he says "I wasn't smart enough to reach 39 and start holding—as a lot of folks do, stop counting.

"This is my 39th year of coaching, though, knocking off army time. I don't want to start holding there again.

"But, back to birthday timing. I wasn't very wise. Sept. 25 just wasn't a good day to choose, not for a coach or athlete.

"When it has arrived in the last 20 years I'm always preoccupied with something else, like Tennessee, Baylor, SMU, Vanderbilt, or somewhere.

"Before that, during the war, I always seemed to be stepping into, or out of a boat, around Sept. 25.

"Let me think . . . back in 1942 I was in Scotland at this time, getting ready for the North African invasion.

"The next year, it was Sicily, at Gela . . . In 1944 after the Normandy landing, Cherbourg.

"Now in 1945 I had a real birthday celebration, at Sea Island, Ga. I was just back from Okinawa. Evelyn and I got the kids and took off for Brunswick.

"I know Coca-Cola folks and a lot of big people in Atlanta think they own that property, but in 1945 the way I was operating the word may have gotten around Ole Shug owned The Cloisters."

Selma Ignored Sept. 25

Jordan, loose and relaxed-looking Thursday after the Auburn athletic family pitched him a brief cake-coffee party, tried to but couldn't recall hometown Selma being unusually festive on Sept. 25 during World War I years, and immediately afterwards, during Warren Harding–Cal Coolidge eras.

Jordan said he didn't remember any flag salutes along Broad Street either, or the Albert Hotel management baking any cakes.

"I don't recall getting from my daddy any yellow sports-model car with a rumble seat, either," Auburn's coach laughed.

"We took my birthday pretty much in stride."

Jordan smilingly accepted in stride the happy affair Emily Foster, his secretary; Jeff Beard, his boss; and Gene Lorendo, Joe Connally, George Atkins, et al., his staff, staged Thursday mid-morning.

There was one jarring note, the timing.

"They knew how hectic tomorrow (Friday) would be around here so they made me 60 one day early. I told them I wanted to stay 59 every minute possible."

Silver Lining There

Jordan was able to pluck a silver lining even from that premature 60-salute. He's very good at that, an admirable trait. Living is fuller this route.

"We had this little party during a break in morning work," Jordan said. "It got our worries off Tennessee a few minutes.

"That's another very awesome crowd of people Tennessee has. Fine material. And what I've observed, and read of Tennessee's 28-year-old coach—28? Hm-m-m. I envy him—impresses me too.

"Bill Battle is very settled, very mature 28. He's a very realistic young man, too. His statements reflect wisdom beyond that beautiful age.

"Of course, I've known, admired and respected Bill Battle for many years. It's easy for me to remember, too, with regret, my valedictory to Bill and his parents when he was still at West End High (and highly courted by college coaches).

"I did everything I could to persuade him to join us at Auburn—short of getting down on my knees and singing 'Mammy.'

"That was a few birthdays ago. Time does fly."

—September 25, 1970

'71 Tiders Meet Demands for Triple-Option Offense (1971)

Los Angeles—Just in case you've neglected homework on the Wishbone or Veer-T or triple-option formation, or whatever one would label it . . . and, just in case conservative commentator Paul Bryant has been conservative recently commenting about Alabama expanding its playbook in 1971 . . . keep this in mind listening to Alabama charging against Southern Cal tonight, or reading about it here Saturday and Sunday.

It's one heckuva nightmare to defend triple-option maneuvers. Houston has been using a form of it for years, considering the game bad if it doesn't gain 400 ground yards . . . Notre Damers brag about stopping Texas' Wishbone last January, but the Longhorns still gained 420 scrimmage yards against the Irish.

It is, however, a fumble-formation deluxe. Texas lost six against Notre Dame, causing the wry, but realistic Darrell Royal comment: "They didn't stop us, we stopped ourselves."

If a team has a slick-handed, quick-footed quarterback, it has a head start to get in the yardage business . . . Alabama has Terry Davis. He qualifies solidly.

It surely takes the heat off an enemy concentrating on one runner, as a Johnny Musso . . . Take dead aim on one back and talented toters as Joe LaBue or Davis can kill a foe, stone dead.

Royal, who hates the pass anyhow, has given triple-option stuff a misleading reputation, contend other coaches, including Bill Yeoman, Houston, and Charles Cason, Monnig Junior High, Fort Worth . . . Royal's success with Texas' ground game, and disdain of the pass has spawned belief it isn't a sound throwing formation.

Not true, claims Yeoman, whose Cougars are deadly upstairs, too . . . "It's a better passing formation than running," insists Coach Cason, who fathered the new fashion.

Tide Fit for Triple-Option

Remember this also, in case Alabama Wishbones, or Veers, at Trojans and probably not to the total surprise of a John McKay, suspicious his coaching friend is cooking something new for him:

Less versatility is needed in blocking up front, though powerful straight-ahead lick-popping is a must . . . Alabama has loaded an offensive line with large, strong guys. They couldn't come close to matching pass-protection grades of small, quick Bamas of Snake Stabler's era, or Joe Namath's, but extra poundage should help in trench fighting here, against Trojan monsters.

Besides, Wishbone-type passing is most effective off the running game after neutralizing the awesome-type rush Southern Cal blitzed at Scott Hunter and Neb Hayden a year ago.

Coaches maintain the key to winning offense is to adapt to players' strengths. If ever a team apparently fit triple-option demands, check Alabama of 1971.

This was, you may recall, directed to your attention in this space last January. We shall now see.

Safety Pins for Hannah

Now, briefly, about the Alabama approach to this game:

Quiet but pleasant flight it was from Birmingham Thursday. I've never been around collegians apparently more serious about a game. Omen? Could be.

Kids are going to be kids, however, and God bless 'em. And there had to be restrained laughter about John Hannah's misfortune. John's some kid, 275 pounds of man.

It's tough to fit his clothes, tough. Frank Baldone, Birmingham tailor, did his derndest. Baldone handles the Bama travel outfitting, red blazer, grey slacks. Hannah's pants just simply split, too tight.

Safety pins came in handy at the sprawling L.A. airport—though experienced planner Mary Harmon Bryant was ready with needle-and-thread on the plane to do the mending properly. Hannah was too embarrassed.

And, speaking further about kids, you should have seen John Musso, Steve Williams and Robin Parkhouse sleeping peacefully midway through the 4-hour flight, on a three-seat row, their heads only inches apart.

"You couldn't get a cuter picture in a kindergarten," one pretty wife, a mother, commented. And you couldn't have.

But Southern Cal is very likely to find those three young men are no longer children Friday night.

The Real Sully and Manly Tiger Defenders Get Vols (1971)

Knoxville, Tenn.—The real Pat Sullivan, All-American, Heisman Trophy chaser and all that, finally stood up in the shadows of storied old

Neyland Stadium here Saturday, arose tall and manly, and drove Auburn 86 yards to a 10–9 victory over Tennessee.

But when Sullivan finally showed a regional television audience and 62,900 customers the great quarterback he actually is, he had to be delighted that Auburn defensive buddies had already beaten him to center spotlight.

Tiger defenders, Bob Brown, Tommy Yearout, Mike Neel and Co., really were more vital to this heady Auburn conquest than was the War Eagles' offense. They had to hold the fort, gallantly fight for Auburn's life more than 45 minutes, until Sullivan finally unshackled a Knoxville jinx spot.

Tennessee was limited to three George Hunt field goals, of 45, 30 and 50 yards, no touchdowns.

Gardner Jett's 28-yard field goal tallied Auburn's first points after a Tennessee 6–0 intermission lead. Harry Unger bulled the last five yards of Sullivan's comeback-to-glory parade.

Jett kicked the deciding point with 2:24 left.

Auburn's defense—naturally—held it right there.

Little Neel's brilliant ankle-tackle of Bill Rudder for an eight-yard loss highlighted Auburn's final series halt of the Vols after they had nearly moved to Hunt field goal range.

Before Sullivan connected five straight passes on the touchdown expedition, Auburn suffered a heartbreaking near-TD miss.

Auburn rolled 73 yards early in the last quarter to a first down on the Vol two. But James Owens fumbled into the end zone at the goal line and that might have shattered a less-dedicated heart than Auburn brought to this one.

The break fired up Tennessee. The Vols crunched yardage relentlessly to the Tiger 14 to a third-and-three situation, Auburn's defense had one deadly shot left. End Eddie Welch murdered Dennis Chadwick running the option and the ball fell free. Linebacker Bill Luka covered it at the Auburn 14.

Sullivan had one more chance. Like a champion, that's all he needed. Terribly off target for a first half which favored-target Terry Beasley mostly missed, Sully was dead on target five straight times, to Beasley for six, to high-catching Dick Schmalz for 23 and 22, to Beasley for 19, to Schmalz again for 12 to the Tennessee five.

Unger took it in from there, bursting through right tackle, through desperate Volunteers, and over.

It was the old ball game. Jett's boot was automatic. He never misses.

After a five-for-18 first half, Sullivan ended up completing 14 for 31 and 154 yards.

David Beverly's punting was important to Auburn defense, too.

He averaged 45 yards for six kicks—though Bobby Majors returned four of them for 82 yards.

Auburn's only effective offense the first 30 minutes was after Owens almost broke the opening kickoff, being shackled heading for open country at the Tiger 32.

Sullivan hit Tommy Lowry for 11 yards, Owens ran 14 on a draw, but Beasley dropped two passes after the Auburns got to the Vol 42. Then Owens fumbled a third-down completion on the Tennessee 34. Jamie Rotella got it for the home club.

Both teams sparred then until Majors evaded four Tigers after Beverly boomed a punt 52 yards. Majors was finally knocked down after a 44-yard runback to the Auburn 43.

After Watson ripped seven and four, Auburn held and Hunt zoomed in his 42-yard field goal.

Majors' 16-yard return of a 56-yard Beverly punt preceded Hunt's second field goal. Majors was stopped on the Tiger 48.

A 15-yard facemask penalty against Auburn helped Tennessee power to Auburn's 11, third and two, before linebacker Mike Flynn crushed Watson for a two-yard deficit and Hunt booted good again from the Auburn 20.

Jett had two chances to put Auburn on the board midway through the second period via a field goal, but Vol All-America linebacker Jackie Walker blocked one and tipped the other.

On the first block, Walker was offside. Jett tried again from the Tennessee 33. Walker's tip cut the ball short of the goal posts.

Auburn had been presented the scoring opportunity when Majors fumbled a punt return on his 32 and Beverly fielded it on the bounce for Auburn.

Sullivan, his aim wild and high, just couldn't hit early targets.

Auburn quickly cut the Vol lead in half opening the third quarter. Opportunity was there for seven when Miles Jones recovered Danny Jeffries' fumble on the kickoff runback to the Tennessee 13.

Henley gained nothing, Sullivan missed Beasley and Henley was held to two on a draw. Jett kicked a 28-yard three points.

Auburn seemed to hold the upper hand the remainder of the period until Henley fumbled a center smash and lost the ball on the Vol 49.

Tennessee gained a 9–3 lead after one first down. Hunt zoomed in his 50-yarder on the first scrimmage of the final quarter.

Auburn revved up a comeback try now. But it failed on the goal-line fumble.

Sullivan had pass completions in the abortive expedition of eight and 11 to Beasley and 18 to Schmalz.

What put the ball on the Vol two was Tennessee interference on Beasley on a Sullivan end zone archer from the Vol 34.

What was left after that was the Tennessee drive which failed, and the Auburn drive which didn't.

Late AU Lightning Sinks 'Bama, 17–16 (1972)

Alabama might still win that national championship.

After what happened Saturday at Legion Field, anything must be possible in zany football.

Where are those rusty "I Believe" buttons, those that flourished around Tuscaloosa? They now belong in Auburn.

It couldn't have happened. Could it? But it did.

The Tigers put the blocks to Bama.

Some 72,386 saw it. They believe Ralph Jordan's Amazins scored all in the last 10 minutes, the man's stretch everybody conceded to Paul Bryant's ex–No. 2 nationally ranked Crimson Tide, already kings of the SEC.

Everybody thought that would be Bama laughter-time, everyone, that is except Auburn's defenders, true architects of one of Dixie's all-time upsets.

Linebacker Bill Newton—who should have had a S on a flowing black cape instead of drab old 56 on a shirt bloodied with red (Alabama red)—blocked a Greg Gantt punt, David Langner fielded the high-bouncing ball around the Bama 25. He kept running. Six points. There was 5:30 left, Auburn six back.

Time for Alabama to receive, hammer two first downs and expend what was left of a gorgeous afternoon, against never-surrendering War Tigers.

Gantt trotted in to punt once more. You've heard about lightning. It strikes, and it can strike twice—if it wears no. 56, or 28—that's Mr. Langner who gave a delayed instant replay of his other TD scamper, this time from 20 yards.

Alabama was still visibly moving when Gardner Jett sighted the extra point kick, but Alabama was dead. Jett didn't miss.

Jett hadn't missed the 10th point behind Langner's first romp, either, nor a 42-yarder capping Auburn's only decent offense of the game, a move from its 20 to the Tide 26, early in the last quarter.

Behind only 16–0, only 9:15 to go, Jordan's field goal decision was open to second guess. Two full-blown touchdowns equal 16 points. A tie would have been victory for Auburn people, though not War Tigers. The Amazins.

Forget now the second guess, Jordan knew best. What he knew was of 100 percent coach-of-the-year stuff.

Alabama had got the game by the scruff of its neck but it methodically hacked up 16 points in 39 minutes.

A Tide defense which yielded only 80 yards looked as strong as Ft. Knox to hold that margin—exactly the Las Vegas spread.

All-SEC quarterback Terry Davis had marched his reds 71 yards into the second quarter for a first touchdown. Steve Bisceglia, game running star, scored from the two.

Bill Davis' extra point was blocked by Tigers, but Bama led 6–0. Bama led 9–0 at halftime, after Lanny Norris intercepted Randy Walls and set up a 24-yard Davis field goal.

Midway the third period, Alabama put on power armor again and slugged home from 78 yards in 10 plays. Wilbur Jackson darted across from the six.

Bill Davis was good this time, and all the Tide had to do to keep alive its fourth national title hopes into the Cotton Bowl versus Texas was to hold the fort.

Auburn just wouldn't hear of it.

A 72-yard Gantt punt downed on the Tiger three ultimately established Alabama on the Auburn 38. One more point could now have knocked out the verdict.

After Joe LaBue got nine, Bisceglia added three for an apparent first down on the Tiger 26. Hold it. A Tider was holding.

That penalty killed first-down hopes because Alabama apparently wasn't going to take air chances, and its ground chances against Bill Newton, Ken Bernich and comrades were now zilch, zero.

Gantt finally missed a 50-yard field goal try, long enough but wide left. Auburn was alive again and went straightway to three points, then boom-boom to 17 and to history books for dramatic comebacks.

Alabama's last legitimate turn with the ball after they couldn't punt past Bill Newton proved that it couldn't throw past Langner either.

Langner intercepted T. Davis' high bullet over Wayne Wheeler's head at the Auburn 42. David Beverly had to punt but was trapped by Danny Sanspree trying to pass from his 47 and a time-out try with a pass could catch the clock before it rolled 0:00.

Auburn had a gold-type opportunity to post the game's initial points in the first quarter.

Terry Davis slipped attempting his first pass, pitched behind and short of Wheeler. Langner was there. He rushed his prize 25 yards to the Tide 10.

After a clipping penalty, three Terry Henley lunges had a first down on the five, but Bama held three charges to no net.

A field goal try was fiasco for Auburn, the snap eluding holder Dave Beck to the Bama 29 where he was smashed by John Croyle.

Alabama did some sporadic gaining all the first half, but without an air threat never threatened except when it scored.

At halftime Auburn had one first down and eight net yards, Tiger attackers ended with 80 yards, 50 rushing, 30 passing, but they are but half the team. The better half won. Doesn't it always?

All-SEC Henley, rush leader also, was limited to 39 yards for 17 carries. Sub fullback Rusty Fuller got 26 yards in six calls.

Bisceglia did 102 yards in 24 hauls. Wilbur Jackson 66 in 12.

Alabama's 16–7 first down edge and its 235 yards of sound-and-fury rushing were trumped by one decisive statistical line—and on the scoreboard.

Auburn returned kicks 129 yards, Alabama 53.

For 9–1 Auburn it's a second-place finish in the SEC into a Dec. 30 Gator Bowl date with Colorado.

The Buffs were favored by seven before what happened in Birmingham.

They like that, those War Tigers, those Amazins.

—Sunday, Dec. 3, 1972

Moment for History, as Hank Takes the Babe (1974)

Atlanta—The reign of Henry the Great began at 9:07, EDT, April 8, 1974. Baseball's new home run king did perfect justice to a high fastball served by well-traveled Los Angeles Dodger lefthander Al Downing. Right in the face.

Henry Louis Aaron crowned the ball over the 385-foot section of Atlanta Stadium's left field fence. A park record 53,775 had Aaron's third of eight standing ovations during the shivering evening going on by the time Aaron trotted by first baseman Steve Garvey, into second base handshakes by Dave Lopes and Bill Russell, and a fireworks cannonade was making like another Battle of Atlanta when Braves teammate Ralph Garr guided Aaron's foot onto homeplate.

It was for history, the man from Mobile's taking of mighty Babe Ruth. No. 715. National TV recorded it, and millions can say, "I saw Hank hit it."

"I never did have my rhythm," Downing was confessing a few minutes later in the clubroom. "When he first hit it, I didn't think it'd be going.

"I was watching (Bill) Buckner (left fielder) and he kept going back, back. The ball kept carrying. When Buckner got to the fence, I knew it was gone then."

It wasn't one of his best shots, Aaron was confessing later, but . . .

"The wind was blowing in strong. I hit it pretty good . . . Tom House (Braves bullpen lefty) said before the game he was going to catch the ball, and he did.

"Tom leaped over the fence and brought it to me—and for that Mr. House will be presented a Magnavox TV."

Class, All the Way

Aaron was recalling his emotion for most of the 400 media folk after Atlanta's 7–4 conquest of Dodgers was complete.

He was class all the relaxed Q&A session. People asked, Aaron answered, direct, down-key.

First, the amazing 40-year-old all-timer wanted on the record, was that stories written from Cincinnati that he had given Sunday's game short of his best were not true.

"I never went on a field and gave less than my best," he said with appropriate firmness. "As I said two months ago, and have said ever since, I did want to hit my home run here."

Aaron had been guessing Downing fastball and Downing fastball he got at 9:07 p.m., EDT, April 8, 1974.

"Probably tomorrow morning I'll wake up and feel what's happened.

But right now to me it was just another home run. No. 1, right now, I'm happy we won the game, and I was able to contribute."

President Richard M. Nixon had been on the phone to Aaron in the top of the fifth, after it happened in the fourth, and the president patiently called again when Aaron returned to the dugout. What did the president say?

"He invited me to visit him at the White House," Aaron replied . . . "No, he didn't give me a time."

Someone wanted to know what about the two kids who joined Aaron's track around the bases after he rounded second base?

"Was somebody following me?" Aaron grinned. "I do remember Mama hugging me. I didn't know she could hug that hard."

Ball and Bat to Magnavox

No. 715's ball and bat would go to Magnavox for five years, Aaron reported, and he was happy "the moment is all over."

"I can relax, my teammates can relax, and I hope the Braves have a good season, finish 1-2-3."

Had No. 715 changed his personal ranking of thrills? He was on record as claiming his 1,000th major league hit was No. 1.

"Tonight definitely changes a lot of things," Aaron declared. "This was a record held by Mr. Ruth for 39 years.

"For years I felt slighted by the awards, so I'd have to say I'd put this one right at the top.

"I think I belong to be considered a great ballplayer. There are many others. I think Joe DiMaggio was a great one. I think Willie Mays was a great one; Jackie Robinson was a great one.

"But I wouldn't say that Henry Aaron should be fourth."

What was now ahead for Aaron, his new goals, and what about a managerial career?

"As for records, I'd like to break Stan Musial's record for hits in the league. I need 119 or 120.

"As to managing, at this time I have no desire to manage. I would like to stay with the Braves. We're going to make our home here and I'd like to work in some way, teaching hitting or something like that."

Did Aaron spot a threat to his home run mark, be it 740 or 750 perhaps?

"I think there are a lot of players who could break my record. Reggie Jackson is one. But to hit 700 home runs a guy has got to play a long time, be lucky and be surrounded by guys who can hit home runs, too."

There had been bad weather predicted in the Atlanta area Monday night and it had rained (close to sleet) in the third inning. Did it worry Hank that the game might have to be postponed before four and one-half innings were completed?

Not at all, he smiled broadly. "I'd gone out and put that tarp down myself after the fourth."

—Tuesday, April 9, 1974

Dad's Wish: "Good Luck, Little-Big Girl" (1975)

Dear Susanna,

Saturday is almost here, to be one of the truly significant days in your life. I'm nervous also.

But I'd bet we'll tread that aisle grandly. It's a meaningful occasion for me too.

When you set the date months ago you jested about testing my priorities. Now you know—as perhaps you knew all along.

Every Saturday in the fall there's a football game. I haven't missed many in your lifetime. But, there's only one daughter. Her wedding is No. 1.

I hope I don't get out of step, or blow a cue, to nostalgia. There are wonderful memories of fun-and-games together.

In the middle of two brothers, your preference vote on activities was a minority one. But, in backyard games, in all seasons, you proved the best athlete in the family.

You loved Rickwood as strongly as any of us, too. Eddie Glennon and Harold Seiler were partially responsible. Also Stan Palys, Bob Micelotta, Howard Koplitz, Haywood Sullivan, Campy Campaneris, Joe Rudi, Rollie Fingers, Reggie Jackson, Vida Blue and Gene Tenace.

The skill and grace of the players, the slow-paced but building drama of the great old game, you found attractive. Also the cokes and popcorn.

Our Secret

It's our secret your comments about boyfriends who accepted your suggestion to check on the Braves while you were at Emory, about how they attempted to explain tactics and strategy unfolding.

You women mystify me. Why didn't you tell them about the artistry of Ted Williams in Sarasota springtime; Tony Conigliaro rifling a runner down at third at Winter Haven; Sandy Koufax unloosing lightning at Vero Beach or Atlanta Stadium? You saw it all.

You watched Hank Aaron at Rickwood, too, the dark evening the tornado dipped nearby and shattered lights and transformers into fireworks all over West End.

Cutoff plays, hit-behind-the-runner, lefty vs. lefty, make-the-first-out sure, you learned after lettered blocks.

Running the bases you knew also, by personal experience. Remember the Saturday midnight a Park Board gatekeeper locked us in Rickwood? You wanted to climb the fence, barbed-wire barrier and all. Your dad was a sissy.

So you and Bud and Schuy ran ghostly bases, à la Stuffy Stewart and Billy Bancroft by moonlight—and weren't the stars bright that night?—until a Park Board attendant was roused in East Lake and came casually to un-imprison us. Y'all enjoyed it. I do now.

Terrible Advice

I hope you've forgiven unsolicited coaching before you ran that 600-yard race at Shades Valley High, too. You had won a couple of previous heats to qualify for the girls championship.

But you made a mistake. You mentioned it to your proud pop, who proceeded to tell you how to win the big one: "pace yourself, save for the big kick, dazzle 'em in the fourth quarter."

You came in third, hardly panting. Your coach underestimated your stamina. You could have led, wire-to-wire.

Memories, memories, Littlest Miss Mighty, and for most of our acquaintances tomorrow it's Auburn-Tennessee, Alabama-Vandy Day. Not for us.

You'll be in lovely white. I'll be in dark, but not really sad.

Good luck, little-big girl.

—Friday, Sept. 26, 1975

Class of '76 Comes On Impressively (1976)

Memorable flashbacks to this state's annual most glamorous, most prestigious athletic social, Alabama Sports Hall of Fame festivities:

Remember this, that blooper-famous Rip Sewell is a double-amputee. Then hear him as he leaves a ceremony which he described as the thrill of his life:

"How about that Jackie Hayes and Charley Boswell? Aren't they remarkable?"

ASHF induction ceremonies have had scores of poignant scenes. Hank Crisp Jr. manfully standing in for his famed dad after a fatal heart attack palled the 1970 banquet.

Jesse Owens recalling his Olympics snub by Hitler. "I don't know where he is tonight but I'm having the time of my life" . . . Mrs. Dixie Howell and Mrs. Pat Trammell courageously fighting tears . . . on and on.

But Sewell's jaunty walk to center stage, and his not unlively step-climbing to his spotlight Friday evening, rates with those wonderful, emotional dramatics.

Bart Starr's masterful acceptance speech won't be early forgotten. Tremendous poise, Sgt. and Mrs. Ben Starr's boy has, and so enviably articulate.

Banquet committee escort John Morris is the only person who knows Starr's blood pressure as the movie screen in the darkened hall showed Green Bay greatness as the former Packer field leader stood in the "ready" aisle, watching Paul Hornungs, Jimmy Taylors, Hawg Hanners, Willie Davises flash to memory.

Birmingham's advertising exec J. D. Ferguson deserves applause for banquet film and slides. He beautifully blended them into Tom York again-professional narration.

Next Year

Same as every year, doubters wonder if there'll be a dropoff in inductee quality come another year. There shouldn't be—though one has to be impressed that an eighth enshrinement, upping the total to 58, could present Leah Atkins, Jackie Hayes, Harlon Hill, Bernie Moore, Rip Sewell and Bart Starr.

One expert observer was guessing Willie Mays, Charlie Finley, Spud Davis, Petey Sarron, Percy Beard, Holt Rast, Adm. Don Whitmire, Fred Davis, Eddie Stanky, Leroy Monsky, Jim Whatley, Cleve Abbott, Clyde Morton, Harry Walker, Tucker Frederickson, Eddie Glennon and Sam Perry would be strongly in 1977 contention.

One has to join the ceaseless coffeetalk during off-stage ASHF hours to fully appreciate the charm of the reunion of the mighty in games.

Joe Sewell telling Babe Ruth tales, for example, confessing that Ruth never called his name in five years of roommating, only "Kid."

Or Jeff Beard rolling off the Auburn that was, Sam Robinson, of his track era, "killing a scrawny, old Vet school mule nibbling grass around the football field.

"Sam never threw the javelin 185 feet in this life except that day, and it hit that old mule dead center."

Harlon Hill buddy George Smith Lindsey could brag about his Goober Lindsey golf show in Montgomery. Last year it netted $37,000 for Alabama's special children.

This year Jasper's renowned comic proposes to donate more to those children than more than 3 million Alabamians . . . Last year we appropriated $50,000 to those kids. Goober's gonna beat our miserliness.

Snider Tribute

Fred (Jaybird) House and his blue-ribbon committee of county and state lawmen handle ASHF transportation and security. House is a former Bessemer High footballer-baseballer, a Snitz Snider man—and "proud of it."

"I'm just now getting enough courage, Coach," House grinned at Snider Friday, "to tell you how much I appreciate what you did for me.

"I've been around a lot of your old boys and we've often tried to think of one of your athletes who's gone wrong. We've never thought one up."

Dr. Bernie Moore Jr. of Huntsville was right. He mentioned, accepting his dad's plaque, that his father never knew his greatness . . . One of my all-time favorite gentlemen, any profession, used "I" less than anyone I've known, man, woman, or child.

Small world department . . . Jackie Hayes was telling of the finest baseball game he ever saw, or participated in . . . It happened nearly 60 years ago, Eclectic beat Clanton, 1–0. Joe Sewell heard it.

"You may be right," Joe Sewell said, "Did you know I played in it, with Eclectic?" . . . Hayes didn't.

One reason Bob Veitch was given honorary ASHF induction might have been for such moves by the exec director as appointing Villeta Layton to Doug Cook's banquet committee . . . She's as efficient as pretty, which is very, very considerable.

Irish Mystique Too Powerful . . . So, "Congratulations" (1978)

My admiration is further deepened today for the general brotherhood of probably the only profession in society today not almost totally corrupted by those infamous seven sins.

Columnists, same as effective old cavalry leaders, have to react to the sound of firing, near and far.

Hottest subject being talked in our local precinct of games today is football polls. And that's what caused the reference in Paragraph One about ministers, priests and rabbis.

Each of those groups—strength to them all—has to conduct funerals. None of which, one imagines, is easy. Eulogy is difficult.

What can one say to Alabama coaches, players, friends, to comfort—yea, even to calm yet-swelling anger—after Notre Dame ran No. 1 again?

The cheering after one of Bama's all-time triumphs was yet resounding when bulletins began ticking in with ice-atmosphere effect, from the Football Writers association; AP, UPI and the National Football Foundation: "The Irish are champions; Alabama runnerup—again."

Who recalls the conquest of Woody Hayes and Ohio State now as sweetly as a few hours ago; the brilliant display of less-talented-but-better-disciplined, sharper-coached youngsters bringing honor to themselves, their state and section?

Friends of Alabama are sorely distressed once more. Total defeat in each poll was stunning. Who remembers second place? Only second-placers—and bitterly.

Most Impressive

Could there have been a more impressive team in any bowl than the Alabama men who utterly dominated a Superdome?

Wasn't the Tide's schedule muscle-worthy?

Were Notre Dame's last two wins—one a last 32-minute comeback against a Miami team which Alabama could have beaten 74–0 instead of 36—all that inspiring to vault it from No. 8 to No. 1?

Did Bear Bryant dodge a heavyweight this bowl?

Did Alabama slump against Auburn and Ohio State?

But, there you are. Bridesmaid. Wait until next year.

And don't you know Bryant would like to trade Notre Dame a

planned '78 national championship schedule (including Rose Bowl winner Washington; Bluebonnet winner Southern Cal; Liberty Bowl winner Nebraska) for those three "prestigious" war schools the Irish dated in 1977 to frolic in points, scoreboard and poll-wise?

Jacksonville and Troy could lighten their schedule, perhaps, with Army, Navy and Air Force. Hopefully, our service schools are attracting excellent future generals and admirals—if they aren't we'd better forget this football nonsense and help them recruit—but times are out of joint for them to attract the quantity of quality athletes each once did.

Hail the King

Ah, I feel better now, having hissed out some trifling steam.

The guts of Bryant's reaction to news that Alabama had been rejected again helped me also: "Congratulations to Notre Dame."

CLASS—with all capital letters.

Don't you know that man was bleeding when he said that, and no more?

Wise men have come unanimously to recommend that type policy. It wins, they say, some day.

Meanwhile, please, brake down any impulses to rant for championship playoffs (impractical under normal tournament procedure, both athletically and academically), to write hostilely to panel members who voted as conscientiously as you would have; or spoil your memories of a truly memorable Alabama bowl triumph.

After getting licked fairly and squarely in Nebraska, one of the finest crowds of kids who ever wore crimson and white made a heckuva charge at a mountain peak.

Notre Dame football mystique proved, ultimately, too powerful. Notre Dame earned that prestige honestly. It had an excellent team, too. Maybe the best.

Congratulations, Notre Dame.

—Wednesday, Jan. 4, 1978

Dramatic Tide Stand Overpowers Lions (1979)

New Orleans—Flashy touchdowns by Bruce Bolton and Major Ogilvie provided points which beat Penn State 14–7 Monday in a 45th Sugar Bowl, but a barehanded, no-quarter-asked, primitive man-against-man goal-line stand probably won Alabama its fourth national collegiate championship.

That "they shall not pass—or run" stand made by men in sweaty red made a classic No. 1 vs. No. 2 confrontation most memorable for a Superdome audience of 76,824 and a national television audience.

It came late, 53 minutes into a combat which went the distance, dramatically. Unlike more than 113 years ago, on hallowed Pennsylvania ground, this time it was Yankees charging uphill toward possible victory, with all the heart and muscle and firepower every warrior owned.

Pickett didn't make it at Gettysburg. He had a mile or so to conquer.

Joe Paterno's Penn Staters didn't make it. They had two feet to go—and two chances, too.

Matt Suhey, 214 and powerful, vaulted one foot on the first Lion try. Mike Guman, 210 and bull-strong, leaped nowhere a decisive snap later.

This stealing from the great Lincoln, it is altogether fitting and proper that Alabama's defense be saluted first for the Tide's fourth straight bowl triumph and an occasion which should stamp an 11–1–0 season with the national championship.

Votes will be gathered today by wire services. Don't bet against Alabama this time, don't wager it'll finish runnerup for 1978 as it did in 1977.

The nation's most famous bowl team, running its record to 16–13–3, never trumped a more formidable defensive foe in New Orleans, Pasadena, Miami, anywhere. It trumped that renowned defense with aces—most of them on Bama's defense.

Bama linebacker Barry Krauss, senior, was chosen to represent that winning Tide unit as "most valuable player," first lineman to be voted that distinction here in 28 years.

Krauss was tremendous—usually is, when games have big stakes—but he had oodles of help on the Tide defensive unit. Murray Legg and Don McNeal had just as many five-star plays as Krauss, and Wayne Hamilton, E. J. Junior, Marty Lyons, Mike Clements, Rickey Gilliland, Byron Braggs, John Mauro and Allen Crumbley were prominent in key situations.

Alabama limited Penn State to 19 yards rushing, 38 carries, and only 15 pass completions in 30 attempts.

Four Bamas had an interception, Jim Bob Harris, Legg, McNeal and Clements.

Bama defenders attacked more consistently than their offensive mates. They commanded the field all afternoon except for one 48-yard State blitz to a 7–7 tie late in the third quarter.

Alabama's offense benefited often from excellent launching spots. But Penn State's quick, disciplined, gang-hunting defenders slammed the door to the Tide except on two occasions.

Alabama carried a 7–0 lead to halftime after Jeff Rutledge floated a 30-yard pass to a diving Bolton in the end zone with eight seconds to go to intermission, and Alan McElroy kicked the first of two extra points.

Then, keeping the chin up, the poise rigid, Alabama slammed in the winning edge with 1:32 to go in the third quarter.

Ogilvie rammed over a pitchout sweep from the Penn State eight.

Bama's first scoring drive went 80 yards in six plays. The push took a minute and three seconds—State proving a benefactor to its foe by taking time out after Ogilvie gained three on first down and Tony Nathan five on second down on a Rutledge pass.

Paterno explained later that he thought his team could stop the Tide and force a punt. State couldn't. Brawny Steve Whitman ripped five then for first down; Nathan 30 and seven, and now Alabama took time.

Rutledge passed from there, the State 30, for the game's first touchdown. The very, very much underrated Bama senior QB, pulled the trigger toward Bolton with a Penn State defender in mid-air to bomb Rutledge.

It was a courageous throw—and a brilliant foot-high reception on the other end by the walk-on senior end from Memphis.

Lou Ikner's spectacular punt return set the table for victory points. With his November broken wrist yet in a cast, the speedy senior from Atmore fielded Fitzkee's 50-yard punt on his 30, flashed through a first wave of coverers and used blockers well to weave 62 yards to the State 11.

Bama caught one of its numerous offside penalties from that point before Nathan took a pitch right for eight and Ogilvie took a pitch left for touchdown. Rutledge made neat serve to Ogilvie after escaping a blitzing Lion.

There were 15 minutes and 21 seconds for Alabama to defend the fort. Marines couldn't have been more effective.

Alabama held the whip hand most of the way. Rutledge went the distance except for two downs. Steadman Shealy subbed for that action in the second period but Penn State's aggressive line hinted it wasn't about to let Shealy get wide to operate so Bryant let more-experienced, better-throwing Rutledge keep the throttle.

Alabama smote Penn State for 208 ground yards and 91 upstairs. Nathan was leading rusher, 127 yards in 21 carries.

Krauss led in solo tackles for Alabama, six. Gilliland had five unassisted stops; Braggs, Legg, Junior and McNeal four apiece.

Junior linebacker Lance Mehl of Penn State had 11 tackles of Tiders and six assists. All-American tackles Bruce Clark and Matt Millen, juniors, had 8—4 charts.

McElroy missed field goal tries of 51 and 40 yards in the second and third quarters. All-America Matt Bahr never got a three-point chance for State.

The Lions had only two close shots at touchdowns. They scored on a

48-yard parade, five plays, after Franco Harris' kid brother, Pete, intercepted a Rutledge pass with a diving catch.

Chuck Fusina threw to Guman for 25 yards on third-and-six, and 17 to the end zone to Fitzkee on second-and-eight.

Bahr kicked point.

The other Penn State threat ended in that goal line stand. Opportunity had knocked, after crowd noise marred an audible change of play by Rutledge and a wild pitchout to an unsuspecting, flattened Nathan resulted in a fumble recovered by Penn State on the Tide 19.

Woody Umphrey punting kept State backed deep all the first half. Alabama had chances to go on attack from its 20, 44, 34, 42, 48, 47 and the State 41 in the opening 30 minutes.

State started series from its 13, 33, 20, four, 12, 20 and Alabama 37.

The last position was after Rich Milot intercepted a Rutledge pass, tipped by a Bama receiver, on the State eight. The Lion linebacker returned 55 yards.

Two plays gained nothing before Braggs sacked Fusina for a 15-yard loss and out of Bahr's kicking range.

McNeal's interception of a Fusina pass in the end zone killed one late Penn State threat—Fusina heaving from the Bama 31—and the Lions messed up another chance to start from the Tide 20 when 12 men were on the field while Umphrey shanked a punt 12 yards from his eight.

The 15-yard tax against State gave Bama new life on its 23.

Clements' interception and 42-yard return to the Lion nine was with 12 seconds left.

—Tuesday, Jan. 2, 1979

Almost Heaven: MSU's Bulldogs Riding Cloud Nine over Delta (1980)

Jackson, Miss.—Lion-hearted, tiger-muscled Bulldogs of Starkville jerked heaven into Mississippi Saturday.

Mississippi State whipped Alabama in football, 6–3.

The crash of many records echoed over the world. Some of that noise was the country's No. 1 team being splattered all over Jackson's Memorial Stadium.

The oddsmakers said Bama was three touchdowns better. Emory Bellard's Bulldogs laughed in their faces.

It was no upset. State won everything in sight, offense, defense, kicking and happiness.

After congratulating his conquerors, Alabama coach Paul Bryant turned philosophical.

"Maybe the Good Lord planned things this way as a test . . . We must use it as a stepping stone to improve, become better people and go forward.

"I thought State outdid us in every phase of the game."

Bellard called it "my sweetest win . . . two minutes of my life down there at the end of the game.

"I would put a flat 10-out on this team—just like Bo Derek."

Alabama had a last-seconds chance to thwart justice—as it has several times in this series. Bama fumbled it away. State got the ball on its own 3-yard-line.

Cowbells rang. Mighty Bama, winners of 28 straight; a record 26 in the SEC and 22 in a row against State, was dead. Egyptian-mummy lifeless.

Big bowl delegates among the audience of 50,891 were in shock, same as some 15,500 Tide ticket buyers who came over for a scheduled picnic party.

State's defense ate Alabama's wishbone for tea-time. The Tide netted only 116 yards on the ground, exactly 100 less than the winners.

Bama's field goal was gift-wrapped. It followed a fumble on a punt by State's Mardye McDole, seconds before halftime, on the Bulldog 35.

Peter Kim sidefooted home a 49-yard field goal. It made it 3–0 until State matched it after recovering an Alabama fumble on its 29, three plays into the second half.

Dana Moore kicked a 37-yard three-pointer. Moore kicked another one, 22 yards, three plays into the fourth period.

It was decisive.

Alabama's four lost fumbles didn't figure in this second State scoring. Freshman quarterback John Bond, superstar of this cloudy, breezy, afternoon, piloted his redshirts with poise and skill 67 yards to the Tide five.

Enter Mr. Moore. Exit Alabama into a rare gloomy Saturday.

End Billy Jackson and linebacker Johnnie Cooks smote Bama blockers and ball carriers as if they were high schoolers. Jackson was in on 14 tackles, three for losses; Cooks was in 16 tackles, three for losses.

Except for a last minute rush from the Bulldog 47, Alabama never mounted a consistent march.

Quarterback Don Jacobs completed three passes from there, to Major Ogilvie, Jesse Bendross and Bart Krout to the Bulldog four but lost the ball on a pressure option.

Alabama had another threat in the first quarter killed by an erratic Jacobs pitchout which State recovered on its 18.

Now 7–1 for the season, Alabama has LSU, Notre Dame and Auburn as a desperate hope to get back into the national championship run.

Georgia has the SEC title locked if it can lick Florida and Auburn. Georgia is 4–0–0 in the league.

Bowl representatives checking State here included Birmingham's Hall of Fame Classic. The Bulldogs might have been willing before the Tide. They suddenly became a fresh darling for several other bowl spots.

Alabama never could get a fire lit on attack. The Bulldogs swarmed from every direction. Until the last two minutes, Jacobs was 1-for-9 passing. That sort of stuff couldn't scare State back from eight men around the scrimmage line.

Meanwhile, against the Tide's brag defense, Bond, 6-foot-4 and 200 pounds, of Valdosta, Ga., wasn't intimidated one bit. He got gobs of yardage from keeper stuff, finishing as game's leading carrier, 94 yards on 20 tries.

Freshman Linnie Patrick was tops for Bama, 31 yards, five calls. Ogilvie netted 30 in seven hauls.

—Sunday, Nov. 2, 1980

The Road to the Top Ends in Pennsylvania (1981)

University Park, Pa.—The road to Paul William Bryant's mountaintop reached from Moro Bottom, Ark., to an acre and a quarter green-grass stage in the golden hills of faraway Pennsylvania.

Uphill all the way, with a jillion stops. Only briefly.

Always upward and onward.

Excelsior.

The very, very poor Arkansas country boy made it up the peak on a dark and misty day which shrouded kingly drama.

This was the day his Alabama football team vowed to earn its coach No. 314, push him to a throne room once thought belonged only to Amos Alonzo Stagg, also a legend.

It was no small challenge for young men in white and red, advertised for greatness two months ago, disappointing and inconsistently mediocre until this second November Saturday.

Penn State, labeled by intelligent and conservative Joe Paterno as "my best team" three weeks ago, had dedicated itself to halting history on its home ground.

Those Lions were rated No. 5 in the country, four points superior to Alabama.

Penn State gave it the gallant go. Alabama gave it teasing opportunity early.

Tiders fumbled, they sinned and were penalized, but they never lost poise or sense of mission.

They joined their 68-year-old coach in greatness. Finally.

Bryant was smiling through much of the mob scene after 31–16 was on the scoreboard. He did his derndest to play down "Me."

Bryant can coach winners, teams and individuals. Couldn't stop inexorable fate.

The man had to be destined to be No. 1, the winningest coach of college football. He also willed it so.

So, look out Auburn, most respected Alabama foe. You're in the hurricane eye now. You represent No. 315, the final Bryant-stand-alone mountain.

Yes, Bryant was happy to get that share of fame with Stagg. What had to be most pleasing was the manner his men won this temporary day of history.

"Players win games," Bryant had droned so many times to make that trite.

Players do win games. Alabama players beat Penn State. Make that ravished Penn State.

This was an Alabama atoning for Georgia Tech and Southern Mississippi shockers. This was an Alabama now signaling for attention to move in with so many Bryant teams who contributed in 10s and 11s and 12s and to 314.

These were Bryant men as calmly deadly as those Bryant men who surrounded Babe Parilli at Kentucky, John David Crow at Texas A&M, Pat Trammell, Joe Namath, Snake Stabler, John Musso, Jeff Rutledge and Steadman Shealy at Alabama.

Bama's defense hinted against Mississippi State it was on the brink of bigness. When it did an encore of its famed Sugar Bowl goal-line stand in the third quarter, forget secret.

This time Bama guts and manhood were even sterner-tested— though not as dramatically. This time Alabama had it 24–3, not 14–7, the national championship on the table.

But Penn State had four downs to make 1 yard this time, instead of two downs. They gained a half-yard in two bullish rushes on Jan. 1, 1979.

Penn State lost a yard in four 11-man charges this time.

These Tiders knew history was looking over their brawny shoulders one more time. They loved the challenge. They welcomed combat testing of what their coach had taught them.

So, the defense was ripe for this test, the kicking game had been for weeks, and the offense rushed up to make showtime unanimous.

Bryant knew they were ready Friday—at least his coaches did.

"Our kids will give us all they've got tomorrow," Paul Davis said Friday evening. "I've never been around a bunch I sense readier to play a big game.

"They know what's at stake in this game."

Alabama men did know about the mountaintop. They climbed it with their coach.

—Sunday, Nov. 15, 1981

More Than a Feeling for Auburns (1982)

Auburn-Alabama Day . . . Iron Bowl Day as Ralph Jordan called it. He was center stage at 25 of them.

The most dramatic afternoon in state sports—and the most emotional.

Add Saturday's show to the classic honor roll: Auburn, 23–22.

There was another one-pointer 10 years ago come Dec. 2.

Randy Walls and John Whatley, Auburn quarterbacks that year, returned to Legion Field Saturday for a private reunion. They shared a hunch.

"We're going to win again today," they said. "By one point."

Mailon Kent—QB of the 1963 War Eagles, who beat Bama 10–8— came back with a special feeling.

"Alabama's gonna come up with something new," Kent predicted, "but I hope we keep doing something old—don't give the ball away.

"Our little guy (Randy Campbell) has been terrific. If he can keep the boat steady one more day, two more hours."

Campbell did. Auburn's lone turnover was after hay was in the barn, the scoreboard fixed forever.

Dr. John Cochran, now Pat Dye's chief of staff for Auburn athletics, was a fullback in 1963, probably the most relaxed gentleman of all the Auburns before the kickoff.

"There's a difference between this team than many others in the past," Cochran put it. "These players have confidence.

"That makes me have confidence."

Alabama had its old warriors back at the scene of more happy days than sad.

Several of them had accepted a command invitation by Coach Paul Bryant to attend a practice Wednesday in Tuscaloosa.

Joe Namath was there, as was Billy Richardson, Dr. Gaylon McCullough, Jerry Duncan and Lee Roy Jordan.

Jordan flew in from Dallas. He walked a Saturday sideline.

Jordan had the faith. His disbelief awakened only after time ran down on the Tide as a light rain began to pepper the playground and Auburn folk wouldn't leave the area.

"Auburn people will be in here until tomorrow," said Bama's legendary defender in 1960, 1961 and 1962 triumphs over Tigers, three humiliating shutouts of the Orange and Blue.

"Can you believe it?" Jordan asked, as if to himself. "A perfect game pitched against us. We couldn't get a turnover."

Scott Hunter, 1–2 as a quarterback against Auburn—the two losses to Pat Sullivan in 1969 and 1970—had fretted before the game.

"I'm wondering which Alabama will show up," Hunter said. "The Penn State Alabama or the Southern Mississippi Alabama."

The Penn State Tide was there Saturday, at least men in red and white that gave the cause their last ounce of muscle and devotion.

"But," Hunter went on, "I'm more worried if this is the last game in Legion Field for Coach Bryant. I hope not."

Another Alabama former family member, who asked anonymity, did not see the classic Saturday match. He did check his scouts as to what went on on Thomas Field the last couple of weeks.

"You're going to see different men against Auburn than against LSU and Southern Miss," he said, early Saturday.

"The names and numbers will be the same. Nothing else. The big man has gotten their attention, finally."

Dye had Tigers' attention, too, since they proudly limped away for a supreme effort against Georgia that was just a mite short of good enough.

A longtime Dye fan told downhearted but spirit-firm Dye that a yet-maturing Auburn team was one year short of stamping home a fourth-quarter victory drive.

Campbell and Bo Jackson and gritty little Lionel James had surged inside the Georgia 15 late, first down, down by five points.

Auburn then jumped offside, had some near misses in four following plays, and that was that.

"Next year Auburn will complete that sort of drive," Dye heard.

"You're wrong," the ex-Georgia farmboy who grew to All-American as a player, student and coach, replied, very emphatically.

"These children grew up today. They became men. I think we're there now."

Auburn was against Alabama, again on a late-chance challenge of Auburn's once-hated dictator.

Bo Jackson dived the final 2 feet over men only, against men only.

—Sunday, Nov. 28, 1982

An Era Is Over, But It'll Never Be Forgotten (1982)

Tuscaloosa—The show is over.

It was a heckuva theater, every minute, every gesture.

There was the entrance, the measured step of kingly command, the star arrived on stage.

There was the stately march around the playground, a one-man parade really.

And then there was the goal-post scene, the bit players eager and active, conscious of that penetrating gaze.

There was his sideline ritual, with rolled battleplan, the maestro conducting orchestration.

There were victories. Many, many. There were defeats. A few.

There was the exit, the face carved from Mount Rushmore registering lordly disdain of whatever the scoreboard showed, chin up, eyes front.

There was his palace guard, escorting royalty through the gathering mob.

It's over—except for one final curtain call, in Memphis, Dec. 29.

Paul William Bryant, Arkansas son of the soil, Alabama's for a grand quarter-century, 1958–1982, is leaving the ring.

He departs as a champion. One year doesn't count. A lifetime does.

That legend doesn't end. It's for history.

Bryant on game day, combat site, was style. Style, alone, won't win. Many losers have style.

Substance will win. Bryant had substance first, discipline and order in himself, then into the boys he'd molded into the men he took to battle.

Always he spoke of class. His players performed with class, if they played.

"Be brave," Bill Battle tells it, "was always the last thing Coach would say as we left the dressing room before a game."

Alabama players played bravely, as did Texas A&M players and Kentucky players and Maryland players before them.

Bryant influenced every mama's and papa's son he coached, the vast majority of those thousands positively.

No prouder fraternity exists—though it's not formal—than those men, now scattered worldwide, composing the "I played for Coach Bryant" society.

Joe Namath is in it; Babe Parilli and John David Crow; Billy Neighbors and Snake Stabler; John Musso and Richard Todd.

Tom Boler and Woody Buchanan are in there, too, and Jim Duke and Danny Gilbert and Sam Maddox and hundreds of other Tiders without lasting field fame. They are also "my chillin" to The Man.

They also served. Bryant remembers.

And more and more, as the years rolled on, and wisdom increased, Bryant, though forever macho, spoke more and more of love to his players.

Sentiment and concern increasingly shared quarters with the competitive fire to excel that flamed inside the poor farmboy Hank Crisp drove into a new world, far from Fordyce, in 1931.

Bryant does care—else why did he demand 100 percent from players? Anything less, he knew, would be cheating.

So, an era ends. There is sadness.

There will be tears today. From Bryant, too. He's not ashamed to cry.

He has to be hoping he made a sound decision. It will be second-guessed.

A generation has turned, another launched since he returned to Tuscaloosa nearly 25 years ago.

Thousands know no Alabama football except Bear Bryant football.

Say this for those: They knew the best.

They knew a coach, but more than that, they knew a man.

The Final Audience for Bryant (1983)

Tuscaloosa—"Paul," begins a white-bearded Duff Daugherty quip, oft-quoted, "you might not be the best coach in the country, but you sure attract attention."

Paul W. Bryant, a few years later was, indisputably, America's No. 1 college coach. He continued attracting attention, and crowds.

Alabama's legendary man attracted final audiences today. They mustered for a last salute in Tuscaloosa and Birmingham.

Daugherty, then at Michigan State, now retired to California, was scheduled to be among them. Early week plans had Bear and Duff pairing for Super Bowl commentary in Las Vegas' Riviera Hotel.

President Ronald Reagan wasn't at Bryant services. He offered to be here, however, to Mrs. Bryant over a Wednesday phone.

"Mama told him we appreciated that," Mae Martin Bryant Tyson said Thursday, "but he ought to stay in Washington."

Billy Graham, world evangelist, had offered, over another phone, to fly in and conduct the funeral services.

"It would have meant Mr. Graham canceling three Crusade services," Mrs. Tyson told it. "Goodness knows, Mama didn't want him to do that."

It was also reported that Graham is recovering from an illness.

But paths, air and ground, to somber-skied Tuscaloosa Thursday had their traffic. That continued today.

John McKay came up from Tampa; Bum Phillips from New Orleans. Charley Pell flew up from Gainesville; Steve Sloan from Durham, N.C.

A private plane from Dallas had another coach, Gene Stallings, as well as a former player, Lee Roy Jordan, and an all-American Bama alumnus, Dave Cowden.

There were Bryant stories told on that airship, one of them by Jordan, who became a Bryant textbook model for courage and class.

"I called Coach not long after the Auburn game," Jordan said. "He told me about a strange dream.

"He said he had dreamed he retired and died a week later."

Bryant Kentucky alumni Jim Proffitt and Joe Koch had not talked with their coach in months. But they came Thursday.

"We're here," Louisville merchant prince Proffitt declared, "because of love for Coach Bryant, respect for his family, and because we want anyone from Alabama, Maryland or Texas A&M to know Kentuckians loved him as strongly as they did.

"There'll be a bunch of us down. Al Zampino, Allen Hamilton and John Miehaus are already here."

Koch is a manufacturer of air filters with sales to 14 countries.

"I knew I was a man after playing for Coach Bryant," Koch said.

"Business was easy after he finished with me.

"And let me tell you this. I was captain of our (1954) team under Blanton Collier, after Coach Bryant left for Texas A&M.

"Every Friday, before a game, I'd get a telegram from Coach Bryant wishing the team success. I'd read it to the team in the dressing room."

Jordan has a host of company from Alabama's Bryant men: Billy Neighbors, Fred Sington Jr., Phil Dabbs, Jerry Duncan, Steve Bowman, Scott Hunter and Benny Nelson in a visiting vanguard.

There were also stories, most starring the man in his various roles as dictator, servant, five-star general, corporal, judge and jury, confessor of wrongdoing.

The world knew him best as Bear Bryant. To his family of men, proudest of societies, it's only "Coach Bryant."

Not once during a long, long day did I hear a former player of Bryant use the word "Bear." Only "Coach Bryant."

Doesn't that tell a story, too?

—Friday, Jan. 28, 1983

4
Final Days, 1983–1990

The final period of Van Hoose's career was a series of good-byes and new beginnings. Bryant's death meant not only the passing of the dominant athletic figure in the state during Van Hoose's career but the end of the Alabama football dynasty, which had carried the newspaper's headlines for so long.

In the first piece in this section, Van Hoose foretells a coming Auburn football powerhouse after the Tigers' second straight win over Alabama in 1983. While Van Hoose missed the mark slightly in predicting Auburn's run, he was among the first in the state to acknowledge that the balance of pigskin power in the state had shifted.

The 1985 Iron Bowl, won on Van Tiffin's last-second field goal, was a final moment of glory for the Crimson Tide, and Van Hoose succinctly captures the euphoria in Bama nation that day. But he wastes little time in upbraiding the national media for failing to properly acknowledge Auburn Heisman Trophy winner Bo Jackson, the man Van Hoose called the greatest athlete he ever saw.

Three of the last six pieces are bittersweet, including Van Hoose's 1987 lover's lament on the end of the last Barons baseball season at Rickwood Field, a place where Van Hoose and his family had spent nearly four decades of summer afternoons and nights. There is the first column Van Hoose wrote upon returning from heart surgery in

1988, which ends as a love letter to his legion of friends and readers through the years.

There are also two columns from 1989, Van Hoose's last full year on the job. In those two, he comes as close as he ever did to controversy in dealing with the first Iron Bowl to be held in Auburn. In the first, Van Hoose argues that everyone is perhaps taking the game too seriously (an interesting thing for a man who worked four decades as a sports writer to say). In the second, he asserts that Auburn pulled a fast one on Alabama in moving the game to The Plains, killing the original spirit of the rivalry.

Fittingly, the last column in this section is Van Hoose's farewell piece from March 29, 1990. In it, he reflects on a life well-lived and a career well-spent, with the admission that he still could have done better. Such self-editing is the sign of a born journalist.

—C.S.

Dye's Tigers Start National Dynasty
Down on The Plains (1983)

The Day After—first hours of next year for the Alabama Crimson Tide.

Auburn is yet in 1983. Its Iron Bowl victory extends a season. Pat Dye's Tigers won the big one, toughly, 23–20.

Neither storm wind nor rain nor Bama men in fighting white stayed Auburn from its predicted move for its second SEC football championship in 51 years.

Has Auburn begun a power run as Alabama had in the 1970s?

Did the Tide crest a couple of years ago? As it must to all the mighty, where humans are involved, is the downhill slide increasing?

No doubt about it, the outlook for Auburn in 1984 and beyond is very rosy. Bluebirds should sing on The Plain.

Auburn isn't about to get up there with the country's elite; the Nebraskas, Texases, Penn States, Oklahomas, Michigans and once Alabama.

Auburn is there. High up the mountain top, eyes on the peak.

A score or so of Auburns played a final game in this state Saturday. They'll move to alumni ranks. But three score or so younger Auburns will be around in 1984, surging into gaps left by the Doug Smiths and Donnie Humphreys, the Randy Campbells and Lionel Jameses.

Auburn has No. 34 back, doesn't it? He should win a Heisman. He has that ability.

And after ABC-TV showcased Bo Jackson against Alabama, the nation has a winter book, spring book and summer book favorite for college's football famous trophy, the one Auburn quarterback Pat Sullivan claimed in 1971.

Hammering out a 10–1 record in '83 from the land's toughest schedule, Auburn should have a less difficult card in '84.

Foes will be the same except that Ole Miss replaces Kentucky and Cincinnati subs for Maryland. But SEC foes Tennessee, Florida and Georgia are home games.

Texas is away. Tough, but an excellent chance for Auburn to test its highest muscle.

Dye has got to locate a quarterback. Gritty little wishbone maestro Campbell leaves the stage after the Michigan challenge in the Sugar Bowl.

Pat Washington returns, but hasn't proved himself. He'll get a chance. So will Jeff Burger, a redshirt freshman.

Amazingly, for a returner, Dye was able to hold out 20 freshmen this season. He makes no secret that group includes at least six offensive linemen with special potential: Steve Wilson, Beauford Perkins, Eric Floyd, Stacy Searels, Ron Tatum and tight end Sherman Johnson.

Alex Dudechock, defensive tackle, sat out the year.

Several other held-out frosh to remember: Edward Phillips, defensive end; Gary Kelley, offensive end; Miles Smith, defensive back, and Russ Carreker, linebacker.

Auburn has experience returning in every position, much of it star material. Bo Jackson, linebacker Greg Carr and defensive end Gerald Robinson dazzling out front.

Alabama in 1984? Interesting speculation.

Start with this: Ray Perkins will know much more about his personnel than he did in '83.

Perkins' maiden season, with the attendant pressure of following Paul Bryant, was consistent with changing players.

He committed many freshmen to battle—Kerry Goode, Cornelius Bennett, Curt Jarvis, Ricky Thomas, Britton Cooper, Wayne Davis and Greg Richardson among them.

They proved they weren't boys among men. They gave as much as they received, oft-times more.

Perkins went 11 games with one quarterback, Walter Lewis. Who'll follow?

Bama's coach said several weeks ago he wasn't worried about Bama's quarterback in 1984. He didn't elaborate.

Two prospects are freshmen. Mike Shula played a few downs, Tim Hecht didn't.

The number one mission for each is to grab the weights in the off-season, and gain strength. They have height, 6-foot-1 and 6-3. They want muscle poundage.

Perkins has been flying all over Dixie courting prospects, including quarterbacks. He can promise that Alabama will throw the ball. For pro-ambitious youngsters, that answers a first question.

Alabama loses a bunch of experience on both sides of the ball. The pitch-and-catch department suffers most: Lewis, Joey Jones and Jesse Bendross will be gone.

The Tide's schedule toughens. It should. Ole Miss ran away, but Boston College, Georgia Tech, Vanderbilt, Penn State, Tennessee, Mississippi State, LSU and Auburn didn't.

Middleweight Southwest Louisiana was signed after the Ole Miss defection. That's a mismatch. Georgia isn't. It's a league-mandated game to be played in Athens.

The Tide also has Cincinnati dated. It should make money on that one—and brighten its record.

Not since Dwight Eisenhower was in the White house in the middle 1950s has Auburn beaten Alabama three years in a row.

The Tigers can in 1984.

Memories Abound from Legion Field's Greatest Game (1985)

There's one in every crowd, 'tis said. This was Alabama's dressing room, heart of the happiest scene I recall since Bill Mazeroski flogged his home run in 1960 at Pittsburgh's now-dead Forbes Field:

Wag to Ray Perkins, Riding Cloud 99, and unabashedly jubilant: "Good show, Coach, for three quarters. Then you let things get dull."

Alabama 25, Auburn 23, violated the great Bob Neyland's almost-perfect dictum. The brilliant Tennessee general-coach believed that "classic football games, like classic battles, are lost rather than won."

Auburn didn't lose. Alabama won.

Recognition of that fact is not guaranteed to cure War Eagle small-houred pillow tossing and replaying. On the other hand, it can't hurt one of the most galling hurts those final 57 seconds inflicted on anybody, any team, any sport.

My memories of the occasion also include Auburn players and Pat Dye trotting from centerstage with heads high, exactly as they are taught to react to more favorable scoreboards.

Class.

Another locker room suggestion to Coach Perkins, earthy but true:

"You and Pat should send your managers back to the field to shovel up guts. Every man out there left everything he had there."

Perkins agreed.

If it wasn't mentioned Friday in the annual personnel-grading guess it was figured as even as any one since 1963.

Joe Namath, Gaylon McCullough, Richard Williamson were Tide aces that season. Auburn had Jimmy Sidle, Tucker Frederickson and superior pass-defender George Rose going for it.

Auburn won 10–8.

An equally close situation existed in 1953. Vince Dooley–Joe Childress vs. Bart Starr–Tommy Lewis. Alabama won 10–7.

Thing that struck me before the kickoff, and confirmed in three hours, was that there was more talent in this year's war than any previous Iron Bowl.

Both sides abounded with athletes of superior physical ability. Think on Auburn: Bo Jackson, Steve Wallace, Tracy Rocker, Freddy Weygand, Nate Hill, Stacy Searels, Brent Fullwood a partial roster.

Think on Alabama: Wes Neighbors, Gene Jelks, Jon Hand, Curt Jarvis, Cornelius Bennett and, of course, Al Bell. Of Bama's top 22 at least 15 were purple-blood high school prospects.

Alabama, as one expert put it, was loaded with "first-round draft choices" (as preppers).

And make no mistake, a high, high percentage of the best college players were outstanding, publicized high schoolers.

A very high ratio of super pro players were blue-blood college players. Walter Payton, John Elway, Dan Marino, John Hannah, Eric Dickerson, on and on.

The point I'm making is that the winner of Saturday's game didn't pull an upset with a mismatch of personnel. Alabama has at least equal talent (on starting units) as Auburn, very probably more.

As usual, offensive linemen got very little ink or microphone opportunity early Saturday night.

That's life. Linemen accept reality.

But Alabama offensive coordinator Jimmy Fuller hugged every interior lineman who blocked for the gifted Jelks or protected Mike (Master Swordsman) Shula.

Fuller's embracing didn't take long. Bama's five starters played every scrimmage down: Hoss Johnson, David Gilmer, Neighbors, Bill Condon and Larry Rose.

It can't be argued otherwise that Pat Washington was, in essence, only a caretaker quarterback this year. He was called from the bullpen after youngsters Jeff Burger and Bobby Walden's inexperience handicapped a new Auburn offense.

Washington wasn't winning pitcher Saturday, but the senior from Mobile had a heckuva finale. As effectively as Pat Sullivan could have done—often did—Washington long-marched the Tigers twice to go-ahead points.

He can live a lifetime knowing that he didn't choke in the heaviest-pressured game of his career.

Bo's Name Carved in Stone with College Game's Greats (1985)

Jim Brown never won one. Arguably, he was the greatest runner in football history.

Joe Namath never won the thing. The game's most celebrated passer wasn't even a near-miss loser.

But Vincent (Bo) Jackson of Auburn University mounted a New York podium Saturday and got to touch a Heisman Trophy, which will put his name in stone for the ages.

Forgotten soon, and good riddance, will be how close the voting. Out of mind, too, very quickly will the amateurish theater which marked the hurry-up presentation drama.

Emcee Bob Costas was running a two-minute offense on the TV show. Jackson got in a couple of sensible answers to lightweight questions and then was abandoned, alone on a mountain peak, for consolation to Iowa's Chuck Long.

Jackson should shake off the artless snub such as he did hundreds of young men on Saturdays past at Auburn.

Heismans overshadow mortals voting for them and giving them away.

The name on each is important. Those names replay history with soft, glowing memories.

Tom Harmon . . . Frankie Sinkwich . . . Doc Blanchard . . . Alan

Ameche . . . John David Crow . . . Roger Staubach . . . O. J. Simpson . . . Pat Sullivan, names like that.

The Heisman Trophy wasn't always sportdom's most prestigious treasure. It is nowadays.

It hasn't had long, either, a really fair election process. Back in 1935, remember, Downtown Athletic Club sponsors simply got in line with their promotion to supposedly honor the best college player in the land.

Other clubs bragged of similar awards. Several across the country jumped into this act later.

The DAC had the New York press going for it, however. That was strong then; it's strong now. And as the Heisman reputation grew, DAC fathers reacted by changing the electorate to assure a more democratic verdict.

Early Heisman voters principally were from Ivy League–Big 10 country. If you know human nature you recognize provincialism creates sectional bias.

Big 10, Notre Dame and Ivy League candidates dominated Heismans for 30 years. Paul Hornung won one in 1956 with sympathy support for his playing on a 2–8 team.

Brown, authoring fantastic feats at Syracuse as he would later at Cleveland, was effectively ignored.

John Huarte of Notre Dame got a Heisman in 1964. He had played five minutes as a sophomore, 45 minutes as a junior.

As a senior he had an outstanding quarterback season at Notre Dame, and a rags-to-riches angle working.

Best football player in the country? Huarte proved a joke. He went with the Jets, then in the minor league AFL, and was an embarrassment third-stringer behind also-rookie Joe Namath and ugly-duckling but competitor Dick Wood of Auburn.

Huartes don't win modern Heismans. The voting panel reflects population numbers of 50 states. Home area bias is not negated but it is diluted.

Alabama Heisman voters—there are 29 in the overall 1,050—got a break with Jackson's triumph.

If the mighty McAdorian had lost, next week we'd have heard howls from Alabamians of red-and-white persuasion as well as those of orange-and-blue.

But a breakdown of the Heisman electorate is open for inspection. The South, really, has a slight advantage if one would carry the one-man, one-vote principle to a couple of decimals.

Forget all that cheer the winner. Bo Jackson will distinguish his supreme award.

Ninety-eight percent of previous winners have played the pro game commendably. Billy Cannon, 1959, is the exception. He went to prison for dealing with funny money.

Some enterprising sports writer ought to research a readable feature on Heisman winners, what happened to them.

Two will be mentioned here briefly, Pete Dawkins, 1958, and Hopalong Cassady, 1955.

West Pointer Pete Dawkins bypassed pro football to accept a Rhodes Scholarship at Oxford, not in Mississippi. He retired a brigadier general a dozen or so years ago and took up investment banking in New York.

Cassady did do a pro football fling. Then he got into pipe-manufacturing and ultimately sold out to George Steinbrenner's business empire.

The colorful former Ohio State halfback now is a player-development exec for Steinbrenner's New York Yankees.

The Yankees once wanted Bo Jackson. Badly, six-figure badly. Will Cassady be involved in the next Yankee romance of Jackson, next May?

Interesting.

—Sunday, Dec. 8, 1985

Saying Goodbye to Rickwood (1987)

I always thought my mother's flowers presented extra beauty because she nurtured them with so much love.

Old Rickwood, though degenerating dowdily through cracked cosmetics in recent years, is a special rose, of sorts, to me. Maybe because I love that place.

It has provided such a grand enrichment site for us through years that have flown so swiftly.

Ah, the friendships bonded there for me on relaxed spring and summer afternoons. Eddie Glennon's memory surfaces automatically. A rare man, bubbling with energy and wit and a competitive fire unrivaled by all but a few fanatics in any business.

Several Glennon managers are particularly memorable, Fred Walters, Mayo Smith, John Pesky, Cal Ermer and scowl-faced Frank Skaff so warm inside.

Haywood Sullivan, a natural leader of men, came after Glennon. So did a really quiet Irishman, John Francis McNamara.

Rickwood introduced me to J. Robert Scranton, one of my top 10 favorite people. It provided common ground for a brotherly friendship with Harold Seiler, a magnificent human being, the most fearless man, mentally and physically, I've known.

There are treasured memories of a rooftop fraternity of writers and radio folk, Zipp Newman, Henry Vance, Bob Phillips, Walton Lowry, Benny Marshall, Naylor Stone, John Forney, Gabby Bell, and of course, gentlemanly Frank McGowan.

Cowboy Rogers, genuine character, was up there too, before Western Union was trumped by fancy computers.

Barons won, Barons lost, but they played only transient games. Time eroded results. Fellowship lasted lifetimes.

So many Rickwood player-alumni surface to memory, Willie Mays leading off.

I was official scorer for Tom Hayes' Black Barons when this unmatched talent was known only to a handful of voting Birmingham citizens.

The first column I wrote for this paper (Zipp Newman was vacationing) stirred controversy. It was contended that this Westfield High kid was a better center fielder than Jim Piersall, one of Rickwood's all-time darlings.

Willie Who? Forget it, smart-aleck kid.

Walt Dropo, the Big Moose from Moosup, who could forget him? Or George Wilson, the bragging slugger, or Bobo Newsom, the fat, foxy pitcher winning a few as he traveled down the dark side of a colorful career?

The year 1958 was historical. Birmingham broke a 27-year slump and grabbed a pennant. Lou Limmer (who fidgeted through Star-Spangled Banners) hit 30 home runs; Little Bill Harrington won 20; Carl Wagner guarded home plate as toughly as Lee Roy Jordan would have and Manager Ermer orchestrated team unity with his fists.

Yes, you're right. I did admire Stan Palys, The Monster, the toughest hitter in a clutch I remember.

Flag-year 1967 was significant by an explosion of talent, future Hall of Famers Reggie Jackson and Rollie Fingers, plus Dave Duncan and a better big-league prospect than Fingers, George Lazerique. Lazerique squandered God-given athletic gifts.

Duty didn't call me to Rickwood Tuesday night. Nostalgia did. Rico Petrocelli's blazing Barons made more big-league plays in a 10–0 frolic over Charlotte than in any game I recall. Second baseman Rolando Pino and shortstop Jerry Bertolani shared five glove gems in the first two innings.

Neither Tom Forrester nor Rondal Rollin flogged a home run. But they, and their mates, are swinging their bats as confidently as Fred Walters' 1948 gang in the Dixie Series against Fort Worth.

It was another entertaining Rickwood drama. There have been thousands. There could be a rousing finale tonight.

I won't be there. I waved goodbye to pro baseball at Rickwood Field Tuesday night.

There were no tears—only, silently, "Thanks, ancient friend, for all the memories."

—Thursday, September 17, 1987

For Prayers, Love, Support: A Sincere Thanks (1988)

Exactly 256 years after the birthdate of a famous first-man, George Washington, an admirer faced a first himself: major surgery.

May I ask, today, your indulgence to report on a few aspects that followed? It wasn't, and isn't, major news but it's significant to me. I owe bills from it, none financial, that can never be repaid.

What led to a beautiful February morning and a man finally recognizing, starkly, his mortality was a test of miracle modern medicine. Three days earlier it had unmasked the cause of a hurting upper-chest and painful left arm: two completely blocked arteries, one almost.

In the so-called good old days of Dwight Eisenhower's Era, and possibly young John Kennedy's, one's doctors would've presented one with soothing bedside talk with no optimistic base.

Times have changed. Scores of University of Alabama–Birmingham star heart specialists were prominent in perfecting techniques toward a wonderful revolution of sorts. The good work continues, daily. Strength to them; strength to their colleagues, world-wide.

So, the day after Washington's birthday, due to the skill of Stan Lochridge's team—he, I'm proud to report, a once outstanding basketballer-baseballer for Bobby Lott at Hamilton High—a new man wasn't created, only a happier, healthier one.

That was the key factor in my story today but not the warmest, most memorable one. That one involved hundreds of people, friends.

An outpouring of prayers, love and support made me a prisoner of debt for life.

A succession of topical subjects when I came back to this space sidetracked formal thanks to so many of you. The tardiness does not imply lack of appreciation.

This forum is taken seriously as an opportunity to maybe enlighten or entertain you about games and people in them. The word "I" is seldom used here without a conscience twinge. Middleman status is preferred, between newsy folk and you.

That philosophy, and space, precludes naming hundreds of special people to me the last 11 weeks. They nursed, they medicated, they telephoned, they sent flowers, morale-lifting cards, goody baskets and trays of food.

It will be mentioned that Bo Jackson had little time in March of 1987 for a visitor to Fort Myers but was lavish with it on a telephone in March of 1988.

He was not calling, he said, "to get my name in the paper. I just hope you get well."

Jackson is not a typical athlete. He's the greatest of all time. His concern was atypical, and great.

There were several notes from people I never met, humans concerned about a fellow man.

What warm reflections this spawns. Nature decrees lower beasts ignore their unfortunates. We higher-order animals are different. We rally round the sick and wounded.

Recuperation time afforded luxury reading time, one book to be reread maybe the 10th time: *Wind, Sand and Stars.*

Twenty-two years ago in a prelude column before flying to Vietnam it was mentioned that my suitcase would include *Hamlet* plus four of my half-dozen favorite books; the Bible, Joe Palmer's *This Was Racing,* Thornton Wilder's *Ides of March* and that Antoine de Saint Exupery matchless classic of style, beauty and sensitivity.

The enigmatic French flier was an author one should read to determine how one really feels in many meaningful emotional and physical crises.

"We forget," he wrote once, "that there is no hope of joy except in human relations.

"If I summon up those memories that have left me with enduring savor, if I draw up the balance sheet of the hours in my life that have truly counted, surely I find only those that wealth could not have procured me.

"True riches cannot be bought . . . happiness! It is useless to seek it elsewhere than in the warmth of human relations."

May I say again, simply, sincerely: "Thanks."

Maybe This Game Is Too Big (1989)

As a wise man commented, "From the mouths of children . . . wisdom."

From the mouth of Jon Martin, son of *News* golf writer Jim Martin:

"Gosh, Dad, I sure hope they don't interrupt the (TV) Alabama-Auburn game with President Bush and Mr. Gorbachev."

How much is too much? Hasn't too much been written and spoken about this football game?

Is my reaction lonesome that I'll be happier when it is over?

My conscience clangs a bell that a ball contest between 18–21-year-olds should not be Armageddon.

No game in this series has collected such intensity, apprehension and ticket prices as this one.

For the first time, I'm receptive to arguments that maybe this rivalry needs a break.

Paul Bryant, an expert, kept insisting in his last years that the series had become too divisive in terms of state well-being.

Of course, anything Bryant said aroused instant 99.9 percent Auburn opposition. Bryant had Alabama doubters also on this issue.

Time may add another star in Bryant's crown as a perception master.

Some History

Auburn's David Housel, eminent in public relations, leaped into history in a release the other day. His account of why the Tiger-Tide rivalry began again in 1948, after a 41-year lapse, has weak foundation points.

"The athletic rivalry resumed not because of the state Legislature," Housel wrote. Technically, he's right. All the purse-holder Legislature did was to tell the schools to re-marry, or else—a shot-gun marriage sort of threat.

Housel presented school presidents Ralph Draughon (Auburn) and John Gallalee (Alabama) as peacemakers without pressure.

Neither merited Nobel nomination. Neither had historic careers. But, fresh at their posts, no established support bases, both understood a power threat.

Gallalee, a Brand-X sports fan, at best, deserves higher commendation than Draughon for the rebirth of Tide-Tigers competition. His athletic director was Frank Thomas.

Thomas was bitterly opposed to playing Auburn in anything—as Bryant was years later about UAB. Gallalee chose to infuriate his AD rather than Montgomery politicians.

Thomas wanted no part of Auburn because he enjoyed his Crimson Tide as indisputable king of football in his state.

If Alabama played Auburn, went Thomas' reasoning, Alabama would be, in effect, subsidizing impoverished Auburn.

Thomas predicted Auburn would use Alabama football to escape the poor house.

It happened. The astute Jeff Beard and able Ralph Jordan did generate income in other areas but the Alabama game was their golden egg. They could borrow at the bank on it.

The schools' kiss-and-make-up was applauded by state citizens. There were only a fistful of pessimists about first-game deportment. They were wrong—modern ones will be about Saturday's first show in Jordan-Hare Stadium.

Have Fun at Auburn

Connie Kanakis, Birmingham restaurateur, heir to intuition of Greek forebears, has filibustered Alabama fans all week:

"Hey, you aren't headed for the Gaza Strip, Siberia, Lebanon. You won't see Noriega or Gadhafi.

"You're going to Lee County, Alabama. It's sort of civilized. You'll be treated as guests.

"Some kids are going to entertain you with a ball which bounces funny. Enjoy it. Have fun."

Looking Back, and Ahead, at Tide-Tigers (1989)

About Auburn-Alabama football, ahead and behind:

Auburn proved its point—that it could kill the Iron Bowl.

Auburn also proved again that it could grandly host a dramatic college football game. The event was carefully planned, details superbly executed for Alabama's historic first visit.

It made mockery of the blustery bluffs by Paul Bryant and Ray Perkins that Bama would never play the Jordan-Hare scene.

Now, what next in a growing colder phase of the Alabama-Auburn game?

The schedule has the next game in Birmingham's Legion Field next Dec. 1. Games of 1991 and 1992 are set there also.

Should the "Iron Bowl" label be dusted off for those contests? No. It's really not appropriate.

Alabama, I'm guessing, will judge it can't concede Auburn an extra home-game recruiting edge. It'll ultimately move the even-year games in the series to Tuscaloosa.

Roger Sayers, Alabama president, hasn't hinted this. Nor has Tom Jones, faculty rep, nor Hootie Ingram, athletic director. I haven't talked with any of the three about this.

But this is an option available to Alabama. There are others. The way Bama high officials play their hands should be interesting.

Start your overall Auburn-Alabama series analysis at this point: Alabama, the eminent football power in this state in the memory of living man, has Auburn kicking in its throne-room door.

Moreover, Auburn's Jim Martin, president, Bobby Lowder, trustee, and Pat Dye, AD-coach, out-negotiated Bama's Joab Thomas, former president, Red Blount, trustee, and Steve Sloan, former AD, as if they were children. Alabama let the Iron Bowl get assassinated.

Birmingham as a site was not the only Bama defeat. The key Auburn victory was the stipulation that, beginning in 1988, visiting schools would get only 10,000 tickets.

Auburn sold out a Class D home card (first six games: Pacific, Southern Miss, LSU, Mississippi State, Florida and Louisiana Tech) because Alabama was headed there Dec. 2.

Yes, Auburn has marketed well the last 40 years, getting Tennessee and Georgia nicely in a home-and-home routine, and once Georgia Tech in that loop. But Alabama has been Auburn's main meal ticket.

Remember Auburn has whipped four straight now, and six of the last eight. Tide people are restless.

Objective folk shouldn't squeal one bit if Ingram elects to gain instant popularity among his constituents by mounting a loud campaign to "do something about the football series."

Auburn leaders solidified their support bases for years on the Alabama-to-Jordan-Hare issue.

Ingram could wax hypocritical, too, as in Auburn folk chest-beating that "college football games should be played on campus, for students, etc."

That utopia has long been buried by piles of money. And Alabama football rates high in state big business. Some pro owners are envious.

Ingram could, very piously, plead "the series is getting too bitter, too distracting, for two great academic citadels." He could cite chapter and verse.

Ingram could campaign the SEC for a substitute for Auburn on Alabama's schedule; he could defend, and probably win, a move to shift the game to September or October.

He could say, with justification, "I'm doing what I think best for Alabama."

Who could condemn that?

From This Corner, Just Once More . . . (1990)

It seems only last month. It was 1959.

Barons were major Birmingham spring and summer news. GM Eddie Glennon was all-year in local attention. He knew just about everybody in town, was an untiring do-gooder in civic and charity interests and was the most-sought layman speaker this side of Philadelphia, his old hometown.

A September before, 48-year-old Rickwood hoisted its first Southern

Association pennant in 27 years. Then, Cal Ermer's crew, future big leaguers Phil Regan, Joe Grzenda and Bob Bruce; former major leaguers Lou Limmer, Mel Clark, Bob Thorpe and Little Bill Harrington; up-the-road millionaire radio-TV dynamo Carl Wagner and others, knocked out Corpus Christi, Texas, in six in a Dixie Series.

Paul Bryant had come home to Alabama the year before, not unnoticed.

Ralph Jordan had Auburn football high-roading as never before, or since: 23–0–1. Lloyd Nix, Red Phillips, Tommy Lorino, Jerry Wilson, Morris Savage and mates had presented the state, in 1957, Auburn's first national championship.

The SEC had the strongest head football coach lineup in history— clockwise around the league: Blanton Collier, Bowden Wyatt, Wally Butts, Bobby Dodd, Bob Woodruff, Jordan, Bryant, Wade Walker, Andy Pilney, Paul Dietzel, John Vaught and Art Guepe.

Russia had a Sputnik beeping in orbit. Jealous, embarrassed America didn't; it soon would.

A Relative Rookie

Dwight Eisenhower, overrated general, was a golfing president.

Zipp Newman, underrated citizen, retired after 40 years as *The Birmingham News* sports editor. Brilliant Benny Marshall moved a step and succeeded The Zipper.

Alf Van Hoose, a relative rookie on the staff (12 years experience), became assistant sports editor and thrice-weekly columnist.

Jimmy Morgan, Bull Connor and Jabbo Waggoner, the city's governing troika, did not muster a parade.

My first column, as I recall, was a manifesto of sorts. Same as Ronald Reagan, I can't recall all I wrote. Whatever it was, I meant it. I was rural-reared to a creed that mandated a man's word as his bond.

One '59 promise is remembered—that I knew the difference between a fact and an opinion and that I'd do my derndest to keep the distinction clear.

So be ancient history. If David Housel was announcing the number of columns I've written since, as he does home Auburn football attendance, he'd probably put it like this: "an estimated 7,587."

And One Final Word

Now . . .

Would I take back anything I've written? Darn right I would. I have spawned foolishness with the best of 'em.

Would I do anything differently? I surely would. A major change would be to express more appreciation to hundreds of players, coaches, administrators, field officials, fans and friends who have so enriched my uncertain, but happy, path into growing-more-golden years.

Would I take a million bucks to surrender my memory bank? No way.

Would I accept a forum to introduce people of strong, uplifting hands in my career? Yes, but this one, today, isn't a proper one.

Am I emotional on the brink of another transitional period in an approaching full allotment of "three-score-and-10?" Somewhat, but I'm more nervous right now trying to write a dignified exit scene. The entrance scene, 31 years ago, was a breeze like off the sea.

So, may it be said simply, cleanly?

To so many, from just one: "Thanks."

5
Denouement, Back to Bastogne and Beyond, 1989

Like many others of his generation, it is clear that World War II was the defining event of Van Hoose's lifetime. He sprinkled war metaphors throughout his sports columns over the years and was often called upon to write reminiscent pieces for the news section on the anniversaries of major World War II events.

Van Hoose returned to Europe late in 1989, less than six months before he would retire and less than two years after recovering from open-heart surgery. His eight-day, eight-part series traces the path of Patton's 3rd Army (in which Van Hoose was a captain and line commander) through the Low Countries (the Netherlands, Belgium and Luxembourg) and into Germany and Austria.

Included in this selection is the opening piece in the series, which chronicles the trip to Europe and Van Hoose's struggle with trying to write about something other than sports after so long in the arena.

Turns out Van Hoose had nothing to worry about. Also included is his anecdotal piece about George S. Patton, in which Van Hoose relays his limited personal experience with the famed general and compares him to some of the dominant sports figures he had covered.

Then there is Van Hoose's trip to Dachau, in which he admits he was afraid to tour Buchenwald, the Nazi death camp that fellow soldiers had helped liberate. Forty-five years later, he comes to grips with the horror of the Holocaust.

Last is the story of Bastogne, the site of the Battle of the Bulge, where Van Hoose won the Silver Star. The piece about the battle is not one in which he hounds glory. Instead, he offers that his heroism—as well as the fact he came back alive—was a matter of pure happenstance.

As stated in the introduction to this collection, Van Hoose never got around to writing a planned book about his life and career. His "Back to Bastogne and Beyond" series is the next best thing.

—CS

Retracing Footsteps Taken with Patton 45 Years Ago

Night flight, going back—The moonlight flight from Atlanta to Frankfurt droned drowsily high over the North Atlantic. A long-ago soldier was going back.

A haunting line by an English poet lilted through his reverie: "Of old forgotten far-off things, and battles long ago."

Tomorrow would be September—45 years separating eras as different as Hupmobiles and Continental Mark IVs.

I refocused on a world at war:

—Four dominant giants, in one context or another, center-stage amid the century's most memorable drama.

—Adolph Hitler, Josef Stalin, Franklin Roosevelt and history's certain darling, Winston Spencer Churchill.

I was so young, a bit player, a spear carrier, if you please. But, ah, youth! How grand. How poignant the memories of it.

A first lieutenant, 24, nervously but steadfastly going to battle in one of mankind's favorite war arenas, the forested mountains and lovely valleys dominated by Fortress Metz.

The acceptance of a stranger by brothers-in-arms, into common hazard and certain tragedy, into a brotherhood of love, unselfishness, sacrifice and purpose.

The insignificance, helplessness of mortal man in an artillery barrage, the sky afire amid an earthquake.

The joy of a dawn, the rejuvenation of spirit after a long, long and lonesome night in a foxhole far from home—light is so magically restorative.

Appreciation of small, taken-for-granted blessings—steaming coffee . . . laughter . . . a song, any song, just the sound of music . . . a bed . . . a letter from loved ones . . . the breath of life.

The plane jetted on. Ultimately it would be circling a gorgeous Rhineland Valley with vineyards in harvest season, dewy grass so green, a hilly forest putting on autumn colors.

An American tourist would soon be retracking his uncertain booted steps of late 1944 and early 1945.

He was very excited, thinking back and to hours ahead—a second adventure in lovely lands. All was quiet on the once much-marched front.

He was teenage restive. In the next nine days he'd try to re-create emotions and experiences of dramatic days that were. He would write of that.

Could he arouse interest in readership in an area not related to formal sports?

Not Optimistic

He wasn't comfortable with optimism. Inescapably the story series would include "I," "I," "I," that most presumptuous of all letters. But it was "I" in France, Luxembourg and Germany 45 years ago, and "I" with stories inside, tugging to be told.

From there there'll be no concrete theme, no balance of war-mongering and waving palms of peace.

Several threads of the human comedy can be identified: Heroism and cowardice, triumph and defeat, humor and tragedy, man the nobleman and man the barbarian.

So much for the manifesto, in favor of a brief dose of history.

It was 1st Lt. Alfred S. Van Hoose Jr. who joined George Smith Patton's 3rd Army on Oct. 6, 1944, as a replacement.

His address would be Company C (Charlie), 317th Infantry, 80th Infantry Division. The 3rd had paused across the Moselle River, south of Metz, a periodic war prize since Julius Caesar's Roman conquest.

His tracks would meander the next seven months probably 500 miles, through the Maginot Line, St. Avold, the edge of Bastogne, across the Rhine at Mainz, Wiesbaden, Kassel, Erfurt, Jena, Nuremberg and Munich, to an apple orchard in bloom in the Tyrolean Alps of West Austria.

No Gibbon

There'll be no Edward Gibbon treatment of the wartime odyssey. Civilization was believed at issue then, but one man among millions was not very influential.

There are eight articles scheduled.

Several interesting Americans will get major attention. First in line, Gen. Patton.

Oh, were there space to present many others, as Chaucer did with pilgrims on the road to Canterbury.

Such as:

Sgt. Woody Leece, Kentucky coal miner, drafted, Charlie Company's most courageous, deadliest machine gunner.

Badly wounded in December, Leece didn't malinger in a recuperation hospital in safe England. He campaigned back, limping, to buddies at the front.

On V-E night, May 8, 1945, this soft-voiced, lovable giant took on a snootful of schnapps, toward fitful forgiveness. Then he terrorized an Austrian village.

The day's mail had news from his wife. She wrote goodbye. She'd found another man.

The next morning, sober, abashed, ashamed, apologetic, Leece was also wounded, self-wounded. He'd shot himself in the foot during his drunken spree.

Ultimately, despite near-tearful testimony from Leece's men and officers, who also had bet their lives for their country, Leece was dishonorably discharged.

Inexorable military law was served.

Such as: Bill Suhada, Detroit autoworker, amateur boxer, heavyweight champ, 80th division.

Suhada spent only hours in combat—each minute charging. He knew no fear. He took three German bullets, at separate times, frontally assaulting entrenched enemies. After his third hospital stay he rejoined Company C in Austria, two weeks after V-E Day.

The most respected soldier of his company, ranking field sergeant, Suhada ranged away one night seeking strong drink.

He halted a displaced person in a country lane, a Russian or Pole perhaps, in shabby clothes, meek and mild. Suhada demanded schnapps.

A witness reported that the DP, horrified by Suhada's scowl and tone, panicked and fled. Suhada shot him dead.

There was no trial. Who counts homeless unknowns? Suhada was transferred.

An Unknown

Such as:

Unknown soldier—not dead.

This was a young American, among a dozen or so green replacements being escorted to dug-in, under-fire Charlie Company on Hill 320, France.

Long-range German artillery overshot front lines, a salvo screaming into the spread-out new troops some 400 yards short of their objective.

Shrapnel slashed one soldier's right-leg calf, not seriously, but temporarily painful—an infantry GI's dream: a million-dollar wound.

The blood flow was checked in seconds, and the veteran escort-corporal told a calm, stoical young man the location of the battalion aid station, not 300 yards back.

The kid went there grinning, duty-call discharged honorably, a Purple Heart now his, and no more war. Charlie people never knew his name.

—Sunday, Dec. 17, 1989

Patton, Soldier Supreme, Lies in Luxembourg Grave

Hamm, Luxembourg—This hushed, serene outdoor cathedral of the dead gave the visitor renewed reverence for life.

A soldier of long ago stood amidst this loveliest of places during a Europe Revisited tour after 44 years.

It was the American Military cemetery at suburban Luxembourg City. No sense of duty lured me there, only respect, admiration and appreciation.

According to an information sheet available, 5,317 Americans are buried here.

Among acres of simple Roman marble crosses are scattered Star of David markers, 127 of them.

Rank and color and creed are not considered in assigning resting places, with two exceptions:

—Twenty-two brothers are side by side.

—George S. Patton, general, is slightly segregated, near a memorial terrace. His military genius wasn't a factor. He was there because his grave could be better protected from pilgrim traffic of millions through the years.

There are 13 American military cemeteries in Britain, mainland Europe and North Africa. The 50-acre cemetery in tiny Luxembourg could be the crown jewel.

No American can visit it without an experience akin to the spiritual. Sentinel trees, birch, pine and poplar, guard rows and rows of crosses.

Patios of roses and even brighter flowers grace the inspiring geometrical lines. It's so peaceful.

I could locate no old friend. I know some are there, young men who bet their lives against the steel of the southern flank of The Bulge 45 years ago.

Time has dulled the edge of emotion about them, but not gratitude for those comrades who sacrificed beyond us.

And in the quiet of that recent heavenly afternoon came memory of A. E. Housman's lovely poem:

> Here dead we lie because we did not choose to live and shame
> the land from whence we sprung.
> Life, to be sure, is nothing much to lose, but young men think it
> is, and we were young.

Historians award but three World War II American generals superstar rank: George Marshall, Douglas MacArthur and George Smith Patton Jr.

MacArthur should have been named first. He rates No. 1 not only by his military brilliance but for his dictatorial transformation of feudal Japan toward economic status of yet-mushrooming eminence. Marshall rates highest honor as the unflappable, steadfast maestro of the ultimate mightiest war machine in human experience.

Patton had no high command. He was always bridled, loosely, by superiors who never had his insight as to the tragic mission of their business: killing people; imposing your will on the enemy.

Patton was a field soldier, the best of starry rank.

Indisputably, he was the most flamboyant, controversial American warrior. Patton was my general in late 1944 and most of 1945, 3rd U.S. Army, France, Luxembourg, Belgium, Germany and Austria.

I saw him twice.

The first time was in early November 1944 near Metz, France. From the back of the truck, he addressed, informally, 100 or so line officers of the 317th regiment, 80th Infantry Division.

His helmet glistened with three stars, his uniform was immaculate, and he had ivory-handled pistols on his hips.

His voice was shocking, high-pitched, almost feminine. His size was impressive, 6-3 or so, dominating. Language was profane, earthy, challenging.

Patton was amidst a pep-talk tour of several-score combat units, exhorting them for one more major effort in an upcoming all-front attack of the Siegfried Line and then a dash to the Rhine River.

"If all your men will fire 100 rounds a day at the bastards," Patton rasped, "the war will be over in a week."

Patton was wrong, by six months. But I'm not sure each rifleman executed his orders.

The second time I saw Patton was the day Gen. Lucian Truscott relieved him as 3rd Army Supreme Commander. Dwight Eisenhower had fired Patton because of loose-lipped remarks to newspapermen about Germans 'and Russians.

As de facto governor of southern Germany, Patton had retained a sprinkling of minor Nazi party functionaries in their government offices.

The German economic and political situation was in chaos. Patton's rationale was that he needed the most experienced civil service people to restore peacetime normalcy.

Former chair-borne generals directing U.S. Military Government policy challenged Patton. Eisenhower sided with them.

Patton had some remarks about Russians, too, then U.S. buddy-buddies. Patton didn't like Communists, didn't trust them. Eisenhower wouldn't take the heat with his most-famous general. He pitched him overboard to a nothing, paperwork post.

Patton was dead in four months. his neck was broken in a very soft, two-car collision near Mannheim, Germany. Early injury diagnosis was favorable, but he died 12 days later from pneumonia complications in nearby Heidelberg Hospital, still a U.S. Army installation. He was 60.

Interestingly, Patton's hospital room is a tourist attraction, identified proudly. I didn't re-visit it.

I did go by his grave in Luxembourg. I did not salute. I did bow my head.

His marker is standard: "George S. Patton, Jr., General, Third Army, California, Dec. 21, 1945."

My reflections on Patton, the views of a low-ranking line officer whose fate was tied to the man's expertise and judgment: I have many.

First comes to mind Thomas Wolfe's beautiful line about lovely pre-war Bavarian Munich. It was said, Wolfe wrote, that on a clear day from Munich one could see the Alps (60 miles south). Wolfe said he never saw them "But I knew they were there."

As mentioned, I saw Patton but twice in eight months combat time. But I knew he was there.

This Californian reared on a ranch not far from Pasadena (which would start a Rose Bowl when he was 16) was a martinet. I respected him.

He wasn't palsy-walsy with his troops, no joining chow lines, no fox-hole socializing. Not his style. He wasn't one of the boys. He was boss.

He had proved his valor in WWI, as the principal pioneer in American tank tactics. He rode a front tank in attacks. Won a Distinguished Service Cross. He took a machine gun bullet in his hip.

Patton was the arch pro in his profession, which was war. He understood that human beings mouth piously about peace, then clamor to fight for the shallowest of excuses, mostly relating to pride and pocketbook.

He understood that pro soldiers are basically hired killers. Patton desired to be the best at that. "I hear a lot of crap about what a glorious thing it is to die for your country," he once addressed 3rd Army troops. "It isn't glorious; it's stupid. You go into battle to make the other bastard die for his country."

In a popular movie, *Patton,* George C. Scott won a merited Oscar portraying his character as a blood-loving battle director. Scott's emphasis was off-center, by many degrees. Patton had to love battle, as do red-blooded human beings if they think they won't get hurt. Combat is exhilarating, challenging, a supreme macho test.

Patton understood that. But I think Patton loved battle best because battles win wars. Winning was a Patton passion.

Patton had the vanity common to great actors. The battlefield was his stage.

War is barbaric. Christian theology doesn't apply. Its basis is "kill or be killed." Patton recognized that. Civilians, in vast majority, won't admit that.

Patton attracted scoffers by his insistence on high dress and discipline standards for his soldiers not shooting at somebody. He knew pride and image are important.

He encouraged identity among his outfits, nicknames, slogans. Third Army people did consider themselves special. As Marines do, and Vince Lombardi and Paul Bryant football players did. Pride is involved in that attitude.

In the summer of 1946 I was assigned to 3rd Army headquarters. Patton was still a presence, though he was dead.

Patton alumni told Patton anecdotes as Bryant players will do for lifetimes.

One story concerned his speed mania. Third Army GHQ was then at Bad Tolz, 25 miles south of Munich, a dozen miles west of Bad Weissee, a famous spa with luxury hotels, none destroyed.

Patton characteristically chose the ritziest hotel in Bad Wiessee as his personal quarters, a once-favorite abode of Desert Fox Erwin Rommel. After each work day, it was told, Patton would tell the driver of his boxcar-ish command-car something like this:

"Yesterday you took 11 minutes and 43 seconds to get me home. Do it 11:35 today."

The route was a dozen miles of potholed bridges-out driving through three one-street villages. Bobby Allison or Richard Petty couldn't have satisfied Patton. Speed fascinated him. Impatience probably killed him, although facts of his Mannheim accident aren't certified.

Then there were Patton–Beedle Smith stories. Smith was Eisenhower's chief of staff, an underestimated power broker in American strategy.

Patton hated Smith and vice versa. The feud could have been a factor in at least two classic Eisenhower blunders, the failure to allow Patton to close the Falaise gap in Normandy and the shutoff of 3rd Army supplies after it broke through to the Moselle in August of 1944.

Military experts, now with knowledge of what Germans and allies had available, recognize if Eisenhower hadn't reined in Patton (Ike rationalizing worry about Patton flanks; also appeasing far-behind British and other American armies), the war could have ended months earlier.

Patton people argue their man was wronged because of jealousy in high places. Patton did get headlines.

Anyway, Smith located a fantastic hunting lodge in Bavaria after the war. Deer and wild boar abounded.

Smith posted the place for his private preserve.

Patton, his old staffers told it, heard about Smith's lodge and immediately ordered an artillery practice range established just outside its boundary.

"Now let the SOB hunt there," 'twas said Patton said with a chuckle.

There also was a tale about a group of newsmen interviewing Patton about a particular division that Patton thought hadn't distinguished itself under fire. It had earlier served in Mark Clark's 5th Army.

How had these troops done for Patton?

"They stunk," Patton shrieked. But, spoke up one reporter, in shock, "we have just come from Gen. Clark and he said the division was outstanding."

"Well," Patton was told as answering, "that's the difference between Clark and me. He's running for president, I ain't."

—Monday, Dec. 18, 1989

Man's Inhumanity to Man . . . Never Forget!

Dachau, Germany—With the commonsense realism of traffic court judges who order major violators to inspect morgues and wrecked-car graveyards, many American generals during and after WWII ordered German civilians to tour Hitler concentration camps.

That had to be educational. I never encountered a German who admitted he knew earlier what went on behind those gray walls with electrified wiring.

What went on in all of Hitler's dozen years as German fuehrer was the murder of about 11 million people, including nearly 6 million Jews. Extinction of people was state policy, for reasons or for no particular reason.

Our division, 80th Infantry, 3rd Army, liberated Buchenwald in 1945. I wouldn't visit its horror. I did tour Dachau, Hitler's first death camp, in 1946.

Recently I returned to Dachau. It's a shock-therapy treatment wrapped in seething anger.

It's an experience that brands itself in memory.

"Tell it like it is," the herd howls—most of us running in the herd.

"Tell it, too, like it was."

All right, Americans. Read truth. Involve yourself in it. Visualize yourself a witness to:

A pregnant woman wrestled before you, kicking and scratching; her belly then bloodily bayoneted . . . your wife.

That bony skeleton, with ugly purple bruise marks everywhere on his tight-skin body, mockingly dragged before you, naked, then booted again and again . . . your husband.

That teenager over there you once cuddled and rocked while singing a lullaby . . . screaming incoherently as she is raped by little, hairy animal-humans of a so-called master race . . . your daughter.

Those pinch-faced kids, with the haunting eyes, whimpering from hunger, being lured from the room with a chocolate bar through a steel door to clang with the echo of eternity—the gas chamber . . . your children.

The glazed-eyed man paraded on stage, a crucifix dangling on a chain looped around his forehead. He's being slapped and ridiculed, his brawny tormentors making obscene jokes and gestures about the sexuality of Mary and the manhood of her son . . . your former minister or priest.

Those nude figures tied onto snowy, zero-cold wooden planks outside. Just plain science-martyrs, that is who they are, numbered experiments to determine how many hours are required to fatally freeze a human being . . . former neighbors.

That collection of caged derelicts, once vibrant flesh and blood. They are now injected test-cases of typhus, TB, leprosy, syphilis, black fever . . . your old church congregation.

Those desperately sick people quarantined in the next room on barewood bunks; crawling with lice and fleas; moaning, writhing, doomed, responding to nature calls into ragged, filthy clothes . . . God's children, all; made in his image.

Shocked? Horrified? Nauseated? You should be.

And you glimpsed only the tip of Hitler's hell: concentration camps. Those lead paragraphs, intentionally graphic, were not isolated brutish accidents of lowly Nazi zealots. They were German policy, Hitler-ordered and directed.

"We will forgive," an Auschwitz victim said later, "but not forget."

Man's inhumanity to man must never be forgotten or underplayed. No visitor to fat, prosperous, friendly Germany on the threshold of the 1990s should go home without inspecting Dachau, Buchenwald, Bergen-Belsen or one of the other 14 Nazi concentration camps.

That is for sobering education, realism, from the keg's bottom: "forgive, but not forget."

Notoriety Endures

My recent return visit included a half day in Dachau. It's a Munich suburb, site of Hitler's first concentration camp, 1933.

The very word "Dachau" symbolizes the whole concentration camp subject. It reeks.

Dachau might not have been the most horrible of Hitler hell-holes—Buchenwald or Auschwitz probably were—but it was a madman's first of a series. Its notoriety endures.

My division, the 80th Infantry, didn't liberate Dachau. We did liberate Buchenwald, right outside Weimar.

What an ironic choice for man's supreme savagery to fellowmen. The Tuscaloosa-size community in Germany's heart, Weimar was Goethe's home, and Bach's and Lizst's. Martin Luther became a priest not an hour's walk from a future Buchenwald.

Weimar's Chamber of Commerce boast is being Germany's Athens, Greece—the country's cultural fountainhead.

In 1919 Weimar hosted a constitutional convention modeled after one in Philadelphia 130 years earlier. It crafted another republic. Hitler emasculated this republic 14 years later.

Did Hitler establish Buchenwald outside Weimar for spite? Who knows?

Anyway, our division freed Buchenwald in mid-April 1945. An estimated 50,000 had died there from a multitude of causes. The guards had fled.

The 3rd Army was driving east toward Leipzig. Weimar was a brief stopping place, as would be Erfurt, Jena and Geera. But, in Weimar a curious order came down to unit commanders, maybe from Gen. Horace McBryde, 80th commander; maybe from Gen. Patton, the big boss:

"Without violating security standards, have all personnel possible tour Buchenwald."

Buchenwald? The name then was vaguely familiar. Concentration place, wasn't it?

Most of Charlie Company's soldiers went. Their commander chickened out.

I did listen to horror-reports; bodies stacked in piles like stovewood; dangling arms and legs no larger than broomsticks; ghostly men breathing with fixed stares; the stench of rotting flesh, everywhere, overpowering.

Emotionally Buchenwald was forever seared into soldier memories.

In September 1989 Buchenwald could not easily be revisited. It's in East Germany, its borders then walled or barb-wired.

Two months later the walls would come tumbling down.

Dachau, in suburban Munich, was in West Germany and thus available for another pilgrimage, this one from duty rather than wish.

On my first visit, in 1946, as I escorted a dozen American newspapermen around 3rd Army–occupied territory, Dachau was as it had been during its 12 years of operation.

Inside gray-brick walls with electric barbed wire and guard houses atop were cramped rows and rows of wooden barracks. The prison was surprisingly small, about the area of a dozen football fields.

Conditions were startlingly immaculate, including the crematorium and gas chambers. The estimated 30,000 inmated there on freedom day, April 26, 1945, were all gone. Only prison functionaries remained.

Dachau had become a sort of satanic shrine. It still is. Its mission is to teach harsh history. Only the original outerwall buildings remain. They tell their own stories, with help from computered film.

Custodians say hundreds visit Dachau daily, but only a small percentage of the visitors are West Germans.

There is no laughter, no song. Only cathedral silence.

"We will forgive but not forget."

—Wednesday, Dec. 20, 1989

Remember the Day Bastogne Was Saved

Bastogne, Belgium—The name rings of steel. Strong and muscular. Bastogne.

Then there is Dec. 26, 1944—no national holiday but a day for history to remember. Not as Bastille Day, as in France. Bastogne Day, as in a forever-American symbol of guts and honor.

It's the day Gen. George Patton's 3rd Army rammed relief through German iron to Bastogne, a battered, Jasper-size Belgian crossroads city.

Remnants of several American combat outfits, shattered by Hitler's last but mighty Western Front punch, had reeled back to Bastogne. They found a 101st Airborne Division marching forward.

There was a quick marriage of will and purpose, an all-American union.

Elite paratroopers and former retreaters forged a 14-mile defensive perimeter around Bastogne. In the next 10 days they bared a bloody chest to everything the Germans could unleash: the Luftwaffe, Tiger tanks, earthquakes of artillery, Waffen SS'ers, thousands of grenadiers.

The Americans never surrendered. They had temptations. One of those is not only legendary—it's flat-out truth: "Nuts!"

Gen. Tony McAuliffe snarled that to one surrender ultimatum. He commanded the 18,000 or so gambling grimly against mission impossible and winning.

It is neither fair nor accurate to call the defense of Bastogne the major key to victory in the Battle of the Bulge. Ultimately a record 600,000 Yanks were involved (an exclusive American-German shootout except for a token British brigade). Glory can be dispensed broadly.

Bastogne personified high courage and character. Americans involved elsewhere in The Bulge never resented extra trumpets blown for Americans at Bastogne. To friend and foe, they earned special distinction.

To Germans, the Yanks at Bastogne represented a cancer in the belly of their mighty push toward Antwerp; to American rescuers they represented a magnet for their swords.

Textbook blitzkrieg rules dictated that Bastogne be bypassed. German commanders, early in their winter offensive beginning Dec. 16, swallowed all the territory around Bastogne, presuming the surrounded Americans would meekly quit.

Hitler's desperate surprise attack was aimed at retaking Antwerp, severing the Allied front and entrapping four armies, two of them American, one British and one Canadian.

The Germans threw 20 divisions at three-plus American divisions to blow an Ardennes Forest gap. Then, quickly, they followed their general attack route of 1940.

Bastogne was a hickory nut the Germans couldn't crack. It forced German supply problems which couldn't be solved.

The battered, beleaguered city challenged the best in Patton. He reined in his 20 or so divisions in eastern France and motor-marched them some 100 miles north to blunt The Bulge. He aimed his premier tank-infantry team, the 4th Armored and 80th Infantry divisions, straight at Bastogne.

Patton's thrust, led by the most fabulous field soldier of the war, Creighton Abrams, hammered through to Bastogne in four days. Infantrymen from the 80th supported Abrams.

A few weeks ago I made my first-ever visit to Bastogne, 45 years ago a brick yard, devastated by air and artillery.

The Battle of Bastogne is popularly perceived as Indians attacking an Old West fort and John Wayne exhorting cavalrymen to stand to the last man.

Not so. Bastogne fighting was not house-to-house in town but mostly out beyond its city limits, in open terrain blanketed by a foot of snow.

Killing fields favored defenders—if they were resolute and motivated. America had that type people. I saluted them then while trying to join them from a few miles away; I salute them now.

Bastogne has become a darling in the tourist business. Americans flock there, like Muslims to Mecca. It's Christmas Eve in a toy store and gridlock in the downtown square every day.

Waterloo Revisited

How emotional it was to finally get there. And so peaceful. There were Patton people who didn't make it to Bastogne.

We did try, valiantly.

For Charlie Company, 317th Regiment, 80th Infantry Division, our Waterloo (Napoleon's, incidentally, wasn't very distant) was a hamlet named Scheidel. I revisited it.

I retraced my boot tracks, this time comfortably, not under the ghastly conditions of ice, snow and merciless cold.

Only one old man, with a limp and a cane, joined me on the only street in town. We didn't speak a common language.

Scheidel got a fiery facelift that fair-skied Dec. 26 morn 45 years ago. Since then, time has walked slowly through the tiny village.

Terrorized peasants, about 50 I would guess, had lifetimes worth of drama in 12 hours. The day provided a panorama of war.

Charlie Company had some 60 men left after a Christmas Eve ambush and after an artillery barrage while marching forward Christmas Day.

Among second-day casualties was a veteran platoon sergeant who, through the gray smoke of exploding death, began screaming. Wild-eyed, he panicked to the rear. We never saw, never heard of him again.

Mail caught us after dark. Corp. Jack Borg, radioman from Iowa, heard from his folks: "Jack Jr. arrived today. Kathy is doing fine. Love."

Steadfastly through the night, from Borg's hole, could be heard: "A boy. How about that!"

At 5:30, in blind dark, teeth-chattering platoon leaders hovered around company commander Bill Alverson of South Carolina.

"Mission: Scheidel. First platoon (15 men) attack frontally; second platoon (about 20 men) take flanking hill north of Scheidel; third platoon in reserve; weapons platoon provide mortar and machine gun support.

"Attack to follow 15 minutes of supporting artillery of HE (heavy explosives) and smoke (incendiary)

"Assault time: 0715."

At 0645, faint daylight, Charlie has moved to snow-crushed hilltop above Scheidel, 300 yards away. Charlies scrape shallow trenches in the snow. Ho hum, another day at the office.

At 7, precisely, shells scream overhead and thump in thunderous bursts in and around Scheidel. The ground quivers. The show goes on and on, one round every three seconds for 15 minutes. The firebombs whistle in last. Smoke puts a mantle over a mini-hell.

Two attack platoons move out. All's quiet until burp guns chatter in the village—how could Germans have lived in that town being murdered?

M-1 rifle fire mixes in with burp gun sounds. Firefight! Charlies are in the open; Germans in buildings. Mismatch.

Burp guns and M-1s argue on the hill above town, Second Platoon area. Wind is quickly blowing away town smoke. Trouble.

Scene clears. Several First Platooners spotted sprawled in snow in edge of town. Moaning faintly heard. Second Platoon can't be observed.

Firing has ceased. The attack has halted.

I'm lucky. I've been a spectator. I know it won't last. German artillery is as certain as a mailman.

I crawl 100 yards to company headquarters. Lt. Alverson is on the radio to battalion. He reports attack stalled. Battalion orders Alverson to revive it.

I prod the CO to ask for tank help from the regiment. Battalion agrees to ask regiment. Regiment says OK, check with tank commander.

Enemy "Nice to Us"

Tank commander is radioed (just beyond second hill back). He says the terrain is not for tanks, "too open." If we'd been in woods, he'd have said "too close."

So, back to radio square-one, prodding battalion to pressure regiment to order us tank support. Success. Tank commander ordered forward with two tanks.

He demands infantry escorts. He gets them, a dozen men, including me.

We rumble toward Scheidel, all guns blazing. Tanks intimidate German infantrymen just as German tanks intimidate American infantrymen. Tank guns spawn fear ahead. We reach the one-street village, half of its dozen stone houses gutted or burning.

Tanks take position to guard south flank. Charlies split to both sides of street. Mop-up time.

Sgt. John Woods commands southside gang; I have northside five. Woods' people cover a house with fire as our bunch moved to it. We execute same procedure for them.

Scheidel is swept in an hour. Majority of Germans evidently escape via a gully into nearby south woods. We capture a half-dozen or so in houses. They happily surrender.

One near-tragedy is averted. In one of my houses, cellar noise is heard through a trap door in the hall. The door is open.

"Grenade," I order Pfc. John Barnum.

"Hold it!" comes a shout from underneath. "Americans."

Four Charlies captured in the first assault are in that cellar, guarded by three Germans.

"Don't shoot 'em," Winton Shelor begs. "They were nice to us."

"Thought I Could Help"

Scheidel is now secure, outposts in place, and wounded buddies getting priority. The first one reached, lying patiently, trying to smile, is Angelo "Irish" Ciarnello, a hulking, laughing Roman from Toledo. One of his shoulders is frozen blood.

"Irish," I say, "you're a mortar man, supposed to be on that hill back yonder. How did you get here?"

"I'm sorry, lieutenant," he says slowly, in pain. "I thought I could help."

Litter medical jeeps are requested by radio. Battalion says they can't be sent, "too risky." A couple of Charlies volunteer to go get litter jeeps. They do.

Meanwhile, German prisoners are quizzed. Charlie's German-speaking Hans Brotz politics each to go bring in any buddies "who want a free trip to America and no more snow and war."

One handsome blond youngster buys the pitch—as have many before him, each returning with one to six defecters. He is taken to the town's eastern edge and released. Walks about 50 yards—to death.

Dug-in Second Platooners above town think a German is escaping. I have forgotten to notify Sgt. Robert Ross, commanding the platoon.

Ross's lieutenant has been killed on that hill. Ross will be promoted four times the next six weeks, the last time to second lieutenant. After the war he will be Clemson University bank director for 30-odd years.

Time then to loot for food, particularly jelly or jam. Timbers are slowly burning in one stone house. That means warmth.

"Served Hitch in Hell"

An old lady is inside, crying, futilely flailing at a blaze overhead in her kitchen. With her arms and eyes, she begs help. Cowering, praying no doubt, in her cellar, she has survived a dawn shelling and a firestorm. Her home has taken several direct hits. Its guts are smoking away.

Scattered here and there are small piles of simple things gathered in a lifetime of poverty. Somebody's war has pillaged her treasure.

She opens the kitchen door to her barn (under the same burning roof). She hobbles into damp straw and hugs a dead cow, her old friend, its stomach gored by shrapnel steel. Her sobbing increases.

Sorry, lady, can't help. No men to spare. God help you.

Must inspect the outposts. In one building Red Heffner, sergeant, is cooking a chicken. The old lady, unforgettable, is eating at your conscience.

You snap at Heffner, soldier of class, about "taking food from these poor people."

"But lieutenant," Heffner replies, "the rooster was wounded."

At high noon all is quiet. The natives have been corralled, given minutes to collect extra clothes, and marched to the rear. "For your safety," they are told by Americans who had saved them from something or other by destroying their village.

During the afternoon there is sporadic German shelling, word having reached back that Americans had Scheidel.

P-51s make a couple of strafing passes over the woods 400 yards to Scheidel's east. Several bombs are dropped. We never knew at what.

Near dark a couple of Germans are caught crawling into town. Brotz gives each his sales pitch. He sells one on the mission.

No need to alert Second Platoon this time. It's dark. In about 45 minutes the German is back—with seven friends.

Shortly afterwards, messenger from company headquarters arrives; "Withdraw from town. Fall back to Neiderfeulen" (about three miles back).

The retreat is ordered. After one routine rite. Mortar ammunition is heavy. Soldiers up front have to carry it. Mortar gun chief Jim Zelensky is told to have his men travel light, to shoot all his shells toward Germany.

It is so done. Zelensky is an old soldier.

He also is an amateur poet. The next day he circulates a war poem that several readers consider classic. It ends with unforgettable lines: "It must be nice in heaven, we've served our hitch in hell."

Zelensky's poem went unpublished. His hitch ended three days later, up the road toward Bastogne.

—Sunday, Dec. 24, 1989

Editor's note: The following column is the only one in this collection that does not appear chronologically. In light of recent world events, the Van Hoose family felt its subject matter and message were especially appropriate.

—C.S.

Who Was This German, Claiming "Our" God? (1989)

Mainz, Germany—On World War II combat trails recently for a first time in 45 years, I was particularly eager to locate several spots dramatic for me long ago.

I found several: a farmhouse in Belgium; a bridge site and a wooded hill in eastern France; a village in Luxembourg.

I couldn't find the site of my first protective hole dug near the Moselle River.

And though I search for hours in a Mainz rebuilt after its bombed desolation of 1945, I couldn't be sure that a beautiful old church I photographed was the one of a memorable spiritual experience for me.

It really doesn't matter if it was or wasn't. It represented the Church Eternal and one God of us all—American, German, African, Asian— and that's significant enough. The memory of his face has haunted and intrigued me for 44 years.

Only our eyes met that day. His were dark and mysterious. They hinted loneliness, yet solitude. We were in church, in an ageless Mainz sanctuary of wartime austerity and charming decay.

Maybe Martin Luther had preached here. Or Dietrich Bonhoeffer, as courageous against Berlin in the 1930s as Luther was against Rome four centuries earlier. Bonhoeffer offered his faith in defiance of Hitler barbarism. It cost Bonhoeffer his life.

Since no one could prove Luther and Bonhoeffer had not been in this pulpit, I could fantasize that they had been. A one-time worshipper could feel elevated imagining they had. Much as my mother's flowers always had special radiance for me because I knew the love she gave their nourishment. I couldn't prove they were prettier, but I felt better believing they were.

The old walls of the structure had defied the vengeful American bombing of the ancient Rhine River town. It was on a hill, as churches should be, high and lifted up.

Not a neighboring building had life. The church's hardwood pews and floor had cracks. Everything had been scoured with loving hands. The sanctuary was very clean.

As the law of conquering decrees, American 3rd Army soldiers could do anything they pleased with a Mainz easily subdued. The authority included things spiritual.

Thus it was that the regimental chaplain notified men of 317th Regiment that church services would be held later that afternoon. They were scheduled for that church so easily seen on the hill.

Charlie Company of the 317th had been decimated since last it had formal worship. Freshly memorable had been an early morning attack of Hill 420, a dominating wooded mini-mountain in the vicinity of Bitburg, Germany.

It lost some 50 men to entrenched elite SSers and to a rocket barrage into shallowly dug-in Charlies by supposedly supporting American artillery.

Many Americans were buried in common cemetery with SSers at Bitburg. President Ronald Reagan was to make news there some 40 years later visiting that quiet and lovely spot.

There's special sadness for Americans killed by Americans. That happened occasionally.

The assault of Hill 420 was repulsed by the Germans after American covering smoke blew away with some 125 attackers on open ground a quarter mile short.

Survivors of German artillery, mortar, machine gun and rifle fire spaded frantically into muddy ground. A far-back American, wishing to help, ordered support from a gimmick weapon just arrived at the front.

It was a tank with mortar barrels as rocket launchers affixed on top, about 60 in all. I'd been in a maneuver several months earlier at Fort Benning, Ga., when the gimmick was tested.

There was supposed to be one inviolable rule for the weapon: never, never fire it over friendly troops.

The pattern of the rockets was indiscriminate.

But this rocket tank wheeled up and unleashed two salvos of death. They whistled to earth not on Hill 420, but into screaming, praying, cursing Americans.

Combat soldiers often prayed. Cynics called it "foxhole religion," but frontline infantrymen marched to chaplain services in majority numbers. Thanks-giving was one reason, fear of the future another. Also, the church was associated with the sanity of peace.

So, on this lovely spring day, knowing one more bloody river was hours ahead, 50 or so rifle-carrying Americans went solemnly to this centuries-old church house in Mainz.

Hymns were sung, prayers lifted, the sermon offered—I've forgotten the text. A minister or priest at frontline services, indoors or out, kept it solidly basic: remembrance of missing comrades, request for peace, divine guidance and protection.

The only humbug prayer of that period that I recall was George Patton's publicized, buddy-buddy sort of appeal to the Almighty just before Christmas. It was for clear bombing weather. The old warhorse, in effect, was asking aid "to kill those bastards."

Early during the Mainz service my attention was distracted by a scuffling in the rear of the sanctuary. An ancient German was moving to a rear bench.

When we stood to sing, he stood. We bowed in prayer, so did he. I peeped. As the chaplain preached, the old man, his head down on his hands on a cane, eyes focused on God's man.

Had the chaplain been perceptive, and flexible, what an opportunity for an ageless text:

"Have we not all one Father? Hath not one God created us?"

I don't think he preached that theme. It wouldn't have been popular. God blesses America first, doesn't he? He should, shouldn't he? We pay him more.

But there he was, a German, the enemy, at our service, sharing our rituals, claiming our God, too—with such a serene face, hinting sainthood.

Who could he have been? My mind wandered. Was this his church home? Had it been here, as a boy perhaps, he accepted a light lit first in Galilee?

Was he wed here? Were his children christened here? His daughters married here as generations of lovers before them in this so reverent room?

Or was he, as character lines hinted in that intense face, one man who never bowed to a Hitler pushing civilization to the brink of a second Dark Ages?

Had the Nazis, after testing this man's steel, stolen his purse and done their diabolical best to rob him of dignity and his good name?

Was he then joyously joining allies, Americans who were destroying his country physically but saving it from itself spiritually?

Or had God the Father directed one child, old and steadfast, to His church to worship with children from afar, for His reasons? All answers twisted into mystery, and the mystery hasn't been solved. It never will be. I tried to talk to the old gentleman after the benediction. He couldn't speak English; I couldn't speak German.

He could smile, which is universal language. And his eyes? Did they mirror a sadness of heaven?

—December 22, 1989

Index

About the Author

Although he spent 43 years at the same job, Alf Van Hoose was not a man limited by the boundaries of his profession.

As *Birmingham News* sports editor for 21 years and a columnist for a decade before that, Van Hoose helped define a city, a state, and a region known largely for sports. He was the writer of record for some of the biggest sporting events and personalities in the state of Alabama in the last half of the 20th entury.

Wayne Hester, Van Hoose's successor as sports editor of *The News* in 1990, said that "To many sports fans over the years, Alf Van Hoose has been the *Birmingham News*."

But he was also much more than the "sports guy," as older generations of Alabama sports fans who read this book will remember and younger ones will learn. He was a man for all seasons, not just those where balls get kicked, hit, or thrown around.